Ceremonial Magick
On a Shoestring

Ceremonial Magick On a Shoestring

Alessandro Gagliardi

Ellhorn Press
Hubbardston, Massachusetts

Ellhorn Press
12 Simond Hill Road
Hubbardston, MA 01452

Ceremonial Magick On a Shoestring
© 2024 Alessandro Gagliardi
ISBN 978-1-7345032-3-4

Cover Art by Fuzzypeg, public domain.

All rights reserved.
No part of this book may be reproduced in any form
or by any means without the permission of the author.

Printed in cooperation with
Lulu Enterprises, Inc.
860 Aviation Parkway, Suite 300
Morrisville, NC 27560

Get Free Access to the Supplemental Video Course

The lessons in this book, particularly regarding the Ritual of the Pentagram, are also covered in my video course. The Golden Dawn's Lesser Banishing Ritual of the Pentagram is available on Udemy. While this book goes into more detail, the video course is useful for learning things like how to intone sacred names, and how to make magickal gestures, which are difficult to convey in a book. Readers of this book are welcome to email me at magick@deeperwisdom.org to receive free access to the course for a limited time and/or a discounted price for access to the course forever. (Discounts vary according to region and the whims of Udemy's pricing department.) Feel free to preview the course at https://www.udemy.com/course/lesser-banishing-ritual-of-the-pentagram/.

Disclaimer

Common sense is a virtue, and one which you should utilize at every given opportunity. The words expressed in this book are based off of the experiences of the author. If there is a suggestion provided which will get you in trouble, then don't do it. This book is only a guide. Remember that we are each responsible for our own choices. Nothing in this book is an order. Even if direction and instruction are provided, it is up to you to discern what is appropriate for your situation.

Acknowledgements

I would like to acknowledge the following public domain authors:

- Israel Regardie, without whose book, *The Golden Dawn*, this would not be possible. The figures for the hexagrams are taken from that book.
- Aliester Crowley, to whom this work is similarly indebted, particularly his book *Magick*, from which I pulled his definition of "magick."
- The Ordo Templi Orientis, from whose work, *The Record of the Magical Retirement*, I borrowed the picture of Crowley giving the Sign of the Enterer.
- The founders and members of the original Order of the Golden Dawn, including William Wynn Westcott, who provided the translation of *The Thirty-Two Paths of Wisdom*.
- Arthur Edward Waite and Pamela Colman Smith, for the Smith-Waite Tarot deck.
- G. H. Soror Q. L. (thought to be Harriet Miller Davidson), whose essay, *The Tarot Trumps,* is included as the first appendix.
- Samuel Liddell Mathers, another one of the founders of the Golden Dawn. His translation of the *Bornless Ritual* is included as the second appendix.
- Aryeh Kaplan, from whose translation and commentary on the Bahir, I acquired the figure of Kabbalistic Tree of Life.
- The Brothers Grimm and their translator, D. L. Ashliman, from whom I acquired the fairy tale *The Nixie in the Pond*.
- Lon Milo Duquette, from whose *Enochian Vision Magick* I took inspiration and a quote.
- Don Michael Kraig, whose *Modern Magick*, I consulted to fact-check the ritual work.
- David Robles and A. Marina Aguilar, for teaching me all of this.
- Heather Awen, for the idea and encouragement to do this.
- The folks at Ellhorn Press, for making this book a reality.

Contents

Introduction i
   Who Am I? ii
   So what is Magick? iii
   Why learn and practice Magick? v
   What is Ceremonial Magick? vi
   How this book is organized vii

Part 1: Ritual and Symbol
The Rituals 1
   The Ritual of the Pentagram 2
   Middle Pillar 22
   Ritual of the Hexagram 32
Divination 48
   Astrology 49
   Tarot 53
   Geomancy 65

Interlude: A History of Ceremonial Magick
Historical Roots 82
   The Grimoire Tradition 82
   Qabalah 83
   Hermetism and Hermeticism 83
   Alchemy 84
   Rosicrucianism 84
The Hermetic Order of the Golden Dawn 85
   The Order of the Golden Dawn in the Outer 87
   The Order of R.R. et A.C. 88
   Subsequent Orders 89

Part 2: More than Human
Inner Work 93
   Active Imagination 94
   Pathworking 103
   Beyond the Veil 115

    Practical Magick 122

Part 3: Conclusion
    WHAT I LEFT OUT 137
        Magickal Tools.. 137
        Elemental Exercises 139
    WALKING THE PATH 139
    BEYOND THIS BOOK 140
        Groups 140
        Books 143
        Websites 145
        Your Self 145

Part 4: Appendices
    THE TAROT TRUMPS 149
    THE BORNLESS RITUAL 160
    THE THIRTY-TWO PATHS OF WISDOM 163

Introduction

This book came out of an instructional video I made a couple years ago explaining the Lesser Banishing Ritual of the Pentagram, or LBRP. The LBRP (as you will learn in the first chapter of this book) is arguably the cornerstone of modern Ceremonial Magick. It has, in a sense, taken on a life of its own and is used in many contexts that have only a loose connection to the tradition of Ceremonial Magick (for example, many modern witches use it). People have invented their own rituals based on the LBRP, but the original stands alone as a lens into a much greater system of Magick. That is what this book is about.

My intention, with this book, is to go deeper into the Magickal system that is used by Ceremonial Magicians, and which has influenced every Magickal system in the English-speaking world since then. I say "every", not "nearly every" or "virtually every" because it has been so influential that, if you ignore it, you're probably using it without realizing it. And if you are intentionally avoiding it, then you are still influenced by it in that you are explicitly trying not to use this system. Put simply, it is ubiquitous because it is effective. That is why so many other systems have used it. And you might as well know what you're doing. In fact, even those magicians I know who do explicitly avoid using this approach to Magick all have a firm grounding in it to begin with.

There are many introductions to Ceremonial Magick. Why write another one? I have two reasons. First: My intention with this book is to provide a complete resource for people with extremely limited resources, mobility, and privacy. It was written with two populations in mind: prisoners and college students. One of the things that discourages many from following this path is the impression that you need incredible resources in order to follow it. It sometimes seems as though the only way one could really follow it would be to be an independently wealthy gentleman from the Victorian era, as were the people who originally put it together. That, however, is not true. Sure, it's nice to have access to a fully decorated temple with all the accoutrements, but it is not at all necessary. Everything that exists in that temple primarily exists as a mnemonic device—a reminder—of that which exists on the inner plane. You do not actually need any of it.

The other motivation for writing this book has to do with my approach. One of the things I found when I started this path was that I would pick up a book and it would say how much more important it was to do the work than to read about it. Then it would go on and on about all this theoretical stuff and only finally get to the practical bit at the end. So I would skip to the end to try it out but have no idea what I was doing. My approach in this book is different. I start right away with providing practical exercises to be performed, breaking them down as we go. I introduce each theoretical concept within the context of how you might use it. In this way, I provide a complete introduction to the theoretical concepts of Qabalah but do so through the lens of practical ritual. My hope is that this will both accelerate your practice and at the same time, keep your interest in the theoretical aspects of the work which, on its own, can be overwhelming, sometimes leading to the question, "But how do I use any of this?" Hopefully you will not be asking that through this book (or if so, not for very long).

Who Am I?

Who is this person who presumes to write yet another introduction to Magick? I might as well start with my bonafides: I was initiated into a Golden Dawn-style Order over twenty years ago. It should be noted that this is a Golden Dawn-style Order, and not *the* Golden Dawn, nor any of its descendant Orders. In fact, this Order claims no lineage at all (though the founder suspects that his teacher was probably initiated into a number of traditions that he does not know about). While some might consider this a flaw, I've come to see it as a strength. I am not interested in who anyone's teacher was or whether the charter for their Order came from a legitimate source. I'm interested in who you are and what you can do. I have found, too often, with Orders that claim a lineage they can trace back to the original Golden Dawn that they seem far more interested in that lineage than they are in actually doing the work to develop themselves, as though they believed that just because they had lineage, that gave them a shortcut. Based on my experience, it doesn't. You have to do the work either way.

This Order was not my initial introduction to Magick, though it was when I became serious about it (dare I say, devoted my life to it). I was introduced to Magick by my parents, particularly my mother. When my classmates at Catholic school got confirmed, I was initiated into witchcraft. I have since been involved in Reclaiming Witchcraft circles. I'm also a Druid in the Order of Bards, Ovates, and Druids. I've also received Tantric initiation in the Shakta tradition in Varanasi, India. My path has been eclectic, but Ceremonial Magick has been a path I've continuously come back to.

So what is Magick?

The first definition of Magick I came across was the one in the book of the same name, *Magick*, by Aleister Crowley. He defines Magick as "the Science and Art of causing Change to occur in conformity with Will." He then goes on to explain that writing that book was an act of Magick. He wrote:

> *It is my Will to inform the World of certain facts within my knowledge. I therefore take "magical weapons," pen, ink, and paper; I write "incantations"—these sentences—in the "magical language," i.e., that which is understood by the people I wish to instruct; I call forth "spirits," such as printers, publishers, booksellers, and so forth, and constrain them to convey my message to those people. The composition and distribution of this book is thus an act of magick by which I cause Changes to take place in conformity with my Will.*[1]

---

[1] Crowley, *Magick*, 126.

I both love and hate this definition. I love it because it encourages the Magician to think of every intentional act as a Magickal act. This, I think, is very good and a useful practice. At the same time, I hate it because it is not at all what most people think of when they think of the word "Magick". Is getting a job an act of Magick? Crowley would say, "Yes," so long as getting that job was "in conformity with Will". But you did not pick up this book to learn how to get a job. Based on Crowley's definition, David Allen's book, *Getting Things Done* (GTD) would be the ultimate book on Magick. And while I would agree that GTD and other productivity tools are valuable to the Magician (and anyone, but perhaps especially to the Magician) I would think it a stretch to consider GTD a "Magickal system".

> MAGICK WITH A 'K'
>
> By now you may be wondering why I spell "Magick" with a 'k'. This is a convention that was invented by Aleister Crowley. On the surface, it is to distinguish it from stage magic. (Though, as I write this, there is a stage magic show in New York called "Speakeasy Magick". So much for that.) Some have argued that Magick is an older spelling of the word, which is both true and false. Before spelling of words was standardized, it might be spelled magic, magick, majik, or various other spellings. "Magick" was actually relatively unusual. Crowley was fond of altering the spelling of words for other reasons though, usually numerological. However, that isn't why I use the spelling either. I use it because it's the spelling I used when I was first learning Magick in the 90s. It seems to be going out of fashion to spell it that way, perhaps in an attempt to distance oneself from Crowley. However, I still like it. I see it as more "magickal", if you will. Outside of the context of this book, when talking about magic as a general human practice done across cultures and millennia, I will use the more universal and generic "magic" without a 'k'. But in the context of this book, I am talking about a particular practice, rooted in a particular time, with a particular contemporary context. And that I call "Magick" with a 'k'.

Think, for a moment, how you would define the word "Magick". Think of what it connotes for you, and what it doesn't. Perhaps write some words down. It may be useful to draw a mind map. A mind map is a simple technique where you take a blank piece of paper, put a word or phrase in the middle (in this case, "Magick"), draw a circle around it, and then think of what other words or concepts come to mind. Write those down, circle them, and draw lines connecting one to the other where you see connections. This is a kind of non-linear word-association technique that can be helpful in developing an understanding of subtle concepts, like "Magick". Once you've done this, you might try your hand at writing your own definition, before reading mine, below.

My definition of Magick is this: Magick is the art of working with unseen or invisible powers through symbol and ritual. I would say that if there is not an element of the unseen or the imaginal, then it's not really what I would call Magick. If there isn't an element of symbol or ritual involved, I would not really call it Magick; it requires both of these. Simply engaging with unconscious images and making them conscious (say, by recording your dreams) is related to Magick, but is not Magick *per se*. Manipulating symbols, as in computer programming or cryptography, might be related to Magick as well, but it is not in itself Magick the way I mean it here. But once you are actively engaging with these powers using symbols and/or ritual (usually both, but not always) then I think we've got Magick. That is why the first part of this book is devoted to Ritual and Symbol respectively.

Why learn and practice Magick?

So why engage in this at all? Well, if we go back to Crowley's definition, "the Science and Art of causing Change to occur in conformity with Will," then there could hardly be a more important endeavor than that! That is to say, if you have any desire to have any agency in the world, then Magick (as he defines it) is for you. But even if you constrain yourself to my definition, *the art of working with unseen or invisible powers through symbol and ritual,* I would say that while Magick might not be for everyone, it is for anyone who is interested in fully engaging with who they are and how they can influence their world. Most people walk through the world with very little sense of the unseen and unconscious influences upon their lives. They react, even when they think they act. While Magick is not the only way to become aware of—and ultimately utilize—these forces (psychotherapy and certain artistic endeavors come to mind), Magick is a particularly effective and direct way to widen your perception and influence in the unseen world. Magick helps you to be aware of what you were once blind to. It helps you to develop agency and align yourself with higher powers, rather than simply being a pinball in a machine.

What is Ceremonial Magick?

Magick (or magic) has been around for millennia. It is older than writing (though it is tightly interwoven with the development of writing … there's a reason we call it "spelling"). Some say it is older than religion. Ceremonial Magick, on the other hand, is a fairly recent development. It emerged from the medieval European grimoire tradition—including elements of both Qabalah and Hermetism—along with a strong dose of Rosicrucianism and Alchemy. This all came together in a group calling itself the Order of the Golden Dawn towards the end of the Victorian Era in England, which became the template for later developments of what is collectively known as the Western Mystery Tradition. The very idea, in modern Paganism, of casting a circle and calling in the elements, owes itself to the Golden Dawn. That isn't to say that the Golden Dawn was the only tradition that ever did this. Native American and Tibetan traditions are both known for doing similar things, though with different elemental attributions. But if you put Air in the East, Fire in the South, Water in the West, and Earth in the North (as most modern witches do), there's a pretty good chance that your tradition got that from the Golden Dawn.

How this book is organized

This book is in two parts with an interlude in the middle. The first part introduces the core rituals and symbols used in Ceremonial Magick. The second part goes beyond these basics to instruct you on how to achieve knowledge and conversation with your Holy Guardian Angel or Daimon, and how to perform acts of practical Magick. The interlude provides a brief history of the Golden Dawn which provides some of the context for the second part of the book.

The first part consists of two sections. The first section focuses on ritual and introduces the three principle ritual practices used in the Golden Dawn tradition. They are: the Ritual of the Pentagram (including the LBRP), the Middle Pillar exercise, and the Ritual of the Hexagram. In each of these, we will explore the symbol systems utilized in these rituals so that you can truly master them.

The second section of part one discusses three methods of divination used by members of the Golden Dawn. These are essentially symbol sets that can be used for a variety of purposes, not just divination. These are: Astrology, Tarot, and Geomancy. Astrology and Tarot are generally widely known and probably need no introduction. Geomancy is much less popular, but has certain advantages, not the least of which being convenience. It is much simpler than either Astrology or Tarot, consisting of only 16 symbols (compared to 78 Tarot cards). It also requires nothing but a pencil and paper (as opposed to an ephemeris or computer for Astrology, or a special deck of cards for Tarot). Geomancy, Astrology, and Tarot are also all interrelated and learning to work with one will provide insights into the others.

The second part is also divided into two sections. The first section focuses on how to become "more than human". In essence, this means achieving Knowledge and Conversation with your Holy Guardian Angel or Daimon. This is an involved process that should only be undertaken after mastering Part I of this book. However, it has the potential to profoundly affect your life for the better.

The last section has to do with practical Magick—that is, Magick which serves a practical purpose; typically to achieve some worldly desire.

Some approaches to practical Magick will be alluded to in earlier parts of the book as appropriate (for example, how to use the ritual of the pentagram for practical Magick, or how to use a Tarot card or Geomantic figure). However, this chapter will go into more detail providing a full ritual template for charging a talisman. This section is provided last as it is only after the other sections have been covered that the requirements will fully make sense.

Part 1:
Ritual and Symbol

Magick goes by many definitions. Part I introduces some important symbols and powerful rituals for opening to these powers. We will first introduce some rituals to get you started. In so doing, we will also introduce some of the vocabulary of symbols that define the Magickal landscape. These will be elaborated in the chapters on divination which lay out how to use these symbols to engage in further conversation with these powers.

The Rituals

This book covers three principal rituals from the Golden Dawn tradition. The first is fairly well known and has been adopted by many other groups. It is the Ritual of the Pentagram, which is arguably the most important ritual you will learn. At its simplest, it is a banishing ritual. That is the way it is commonly used, but it is also a great deal more than that. There are many ways to banish evil spirits, so why is this the method that has become so popular? It's because it's not just a banishing ritual. It creates a kind of alchemical alembic, balanced with the divine forces. It creates a sacred space that is conducive to peace and personal development. If all you get out of this book is an effective mastery of this ritual, this book will have served its purpose.

The second ritual (or practice, actually) is called the Middle Pillar exercise. It's not really a ritual like the others, but it's included in this section as it is often practiced along with the other rituals. The Middle Pillar exercise takes one of the elements in the Ritual of the Pentagram and expands on it. If the Ritual of the Pentagram establishes a vessel, the Middle Pillar helps to infuse it with Light. This exercise is effective for drawing the divine into your body and activating the god-like aspects of your Self.

The third ritual is the Ritual of the Hexagram. While the Ritual of the Pentagram is terrestrial, the Ritual of the Hexagram is celestial. That is, it has to do with the stars and planets. It is effective in balancing astrological influences and in calling upon them for aid.

Throughout these three rituals, we'll break down each section, explaining the meaning behind it and how it works. By doing so, you will not only get a strong grounding in these three rituals, but also in the system of Magick itself. This will be expanded on in the second section of this part which deals with systems of divination.

The Ritual of the Pentagram

The ritual of the pentagram is foundational to the Golden Dawn system of Ceremonial Magick. It captures the essence of the system in a way that can be easily done on a daily basis (and should be). It consists of four parts:

1. The Qabalistic Cross
2. Formulation of the Pentagrams
3. Evocation of the Archangels
4. The Qabalistic Cross (again)

Each of these uses parts of the system. This creates a unified whole. It is a powerful and effective ritual. The Qabalistic Cross aligns the magician's Will with the Divine Will, invoking the Qabalistic Tree of Life into the magician's body. The Pentagrams combine the symbol of the pentagram with names of God, charging and warding the space. Calling on the Angels strengthens the space. We close with the Qabalistic Cross at the end, which centers and grounds the Magician.

The Qabalistic Cross

The Qabalistic Cross, like most of the ceremony, is performed using the Hebrew words. The words are, "Atah, Malkhut, ve-Gevurah, ve-Gedulah, le Olam, Amen" which translates to "Thine is the Kingdom, and the Power, and the Glory, forever and ever, Amen." Some might recognize this as the last line in the Lord's Prayer or "Our Father". There is some speculation that whoever added these words was familiar with Qabalah, as the words, "Atah," "Malkhut," "Gevurah" and "Gedulah" refer to the cardinal sephirot on the Qabalistic Tree of Life and activate them in the aura of the Magician.

> ### A Note on Hebrew Transliteration
>
> Hebrew is one of several Magickal languages and the one that is principally used in this book. Like most Magickal languages, it is not written using the Latin alphabet. It is also written from right to left. Since most of my readers probably can't read Hebrew, I have transliterated these words and names into the Latin alphabet, but this poses a small problem. The way Hebrew is rendered in the Latin alphabet is not always consistent, and people don't always agree on how it should be done. Recall the difference between "Kabbalah" and "Qabalah" in the introduction. Hermeticists prefer the latter because it retains the distinction between Kaph (כ) and Qoph (ק), both of which make the hard /k/ sound.
>
> It gets more confusing because different dialects of Hebrew pronounce words differently. For example, the letter Tav (ת) is pronounced like /t/ in the Sephardic dialect but like /s/ in the Ashkenazic dialect. Here we will stick to /t/ as that's what's used in modern Hebrew. However, it gets worse. Golden Dawn authors, in attempting to distinguish Tav (ת) from Tet (ט), both pronounced /t/, would transliterate the former as "Th". So you will often see מלכות rendered as Malkuth. This has led many students of the Golden Dawn system of Magick to mispronounce Malkhut, ending it with a /th/ sound. In other words, Malkhut and Malkhus would both be correct (the latter being the Ashkenazic pronunciation). But so far as I know, no proper Hebrew dialect pronounces it Malkuth.
>
> One other note on Hebrew transliteration: sometimes letters change pronunciation based on context. The most poignant example of this is the letter Bet (ב) which, when found at the beginning of a word, is pronounced with a /b/ sound, but when in the middle of the word, it often (but not always) takes on the /v/ sound. This is why I spell גבריאל as "Gavriel" instead

of "Gabriel". In this case, I would not say that "Gabriel" is incorrect, because that is the archangel's name in English and many other languages. However, I have found that using the Hebrew pronunciation helps me get into a more Magickal frame of mind, so I prefer "Gavriel" to "Gabriel". You can use either.

I have tried to provide both transliterations when it's not too cumbersome to do so. One final note, however: in the end, it doesn't really matter how you pronounce it. You do not need to learn the proper pronunciation of Hebrew in order to be an effective Magician. I will provide the proper pronunciation to the best of my ability as it is how I work, and I find it respectful to at least try to pronounce it the way that natural speakers of the language would understand it. But it will work just the same whether you say "atah, malkhut, ve-gevurah, ve-gedulah" or "atah, malkuth, ve-geburah, ve-gedulah."

The Qabalistic Tree of Life

The Qabalistic Tree of Life is like a map of the divine and simultaneously a map of the soul. As the Emerald Tablet of Hermes puts it, "that which is above is as that which is below." Or as the teachings of the Hindu philosophy of Vedanta puts it, "Atman (Soul) = Brahman (God)".

The problem with saying "Atman is Brahman" is that it does not distinguish between different parts of the self, much less different aspects of the divine. This is what the Tree of Life gives us. The Tree of Life describes 10 different aspects of the divine reaching from the Crown (manifesting just above the head) to the Kingdom (or Malkhut) where you are standing. In addition to an up-down dimension, there is also a left-right distinction involving three pillars. The pillar on the left is called the Pillar of Severity and is manifested primarily as Power (or "Gevurah"). The pillar on the right is called the Pillar of Mercy and is manifested as Glory (or "Gedulah").

We will go more into the subtleties of the Tree of Life in the chapter on the Middle Pillar, but for now, suffice it to say that performing the

Qabalistic Cross draws forth the primordial qualities of the divine creator within the aura of the Magician, empowering them to work Magick.

Performing the Qabalistic Cross

As with most Ceremonial Magick, the performance of the Qabalistic Cross involves two components: gesture and intonation, or sacred speech, particularly vibration. Either or both can be done in the imagination, that is, astrally. It is always better to do it physically as well as astrally.

As an aside, one could do it physically but not astrally, by doing it mindlessly, without intention. This has little if any value. Your Will is what is key here. The body becomes a Magickal tool when utilized in this form. It is a powerful tool, but not an essential one. All Magick can be done with the mind alone, if properly trained.

Intonation

As stated above, the words for this ritual are brief. They are: "Atah, Malkhut, ve-Gevurah, ve-Gedulah, le Olam, Amen" which translates to "Thine is the Kingdom, and the Power, and the Glory, forever and ever, Amen." Each word is, in itself, a word of power. It is spoken in Hebrew, one of the ancient Magickal languages and the one that is most potent in the Western world. Hebrew is so potent a Magickal language that it is found in other Magickal languages in the ancient near east (often in a corrupted form). Magicians from throughout the region, even those who were not Jewish or Christian, would use these words because of the essential power they possess.

Ideally, each word should be "vibrated" with the whole body. That is to say that it should be intoned in a way that causes the body to vibrate. This requires some practice and will probably feel weird at first. I've heard it suggested that you start by simply chanting the word *as loudly as you can*, and as slowly as you can. Each word is a complete breath. You may wish to practice with the word "Amen" (or "Aum"). With its vowels and nasal consonants (M and N), it is particularly suited for vibration.

Even if you cannot vibrate (either because you haven't yet mastered the technique, or you don't have the privacy that would allow you to intone loudly without complaint) you may still visualize the word vibrating through your body, even if you have to speak it silently. When doing so, it is best to visualize it using the Hebrew letters which have a Magickal quality of their own.

אתה	–	*Atah* (Thou Art)
מלכות	–	*Malkhut* (the Kingdom)
וגבורה	–	*ve-Gevurah* (and the Power)
וגדולה	–	*ve-Gedulah* (and the Glory)
לעלם אמן	–	*le Olam Amen* (Forever, Amen)

Gesture

In English, we have a number of loan words from the magical language of India, Sanskrit, for sacred gesture and posture such as *mudra* and *asana*. The Sanskrit term that would most apply to what we're doing here is *nyasa*, which describes placing the god on the body, but you don't need to go to India to see this practice.

When performing the Qabalistic Cross, one literally crosses themself with their hands. It is closely related to the Christian practice of the cross, but slightly different, particularly in the first part.

Begin by standing, preferably facing East.

> ### Concerning "East"
> In nearly all rituals in the Golden Dawn tradition, you are to start and end facing East. However, there is a distinction between ritual East and actual East. This is true of many temples and churches as well. Traditionally, they would be oriented East-West. This is where we get the verb "to orient", which literally means "to East" (or to face East). In real life, this is rarely practical, so in most temples, the space furthest from the entrance is considered "East". In your own space, you will most likely want to do something similar. It may be the wall furthest from the door, the wall that has a window. Generally, the length

> of the room should be "East-West", meaning that East should be one of the shorter walls. But the important thing is that it should be the direction that "feels right" when doing ritual. Throughout this book, when I refer to East, or any of the directions, it is relative to "ritual East" (which may not be actual East).

Inhale, raising your dominant hand (your right hand, if you are right-handed) above your head. This is when you intone "Atah" (אתה). As you do so, imagine yourself reaching up above the heavens into the limitless light (Ain Sof Aur) and drawing that light down into the top of your head, touching the center of your forehead (your "third eye").

Inhale as you draw the light down to your heart or solar plexus and in a continuous motion, draw the light downward intoning "Malkhut" (מלכות), your hand to your groin and visualizing it going all the way through your feet and into the Earth. You are now standing on the central column, or Middle Pillar, extending infinitely in both directions.

Inhale as you draw your hand back up to your heart. Exhale and intone "ve-Gevurah" (וגבורה) while drawing one arm of the cross of light from your chest into your shoulder. Note that unlike with "Atah" and "Malkhut", this placement does *not* extend infinitely to the North, but ends in your shoulder. However, you may visualize a second pillar running infinitely up and down through your arm.

> **IS GEVURAH ON THE LEFT OR THE RIGHT?**
>
> In the Golden Dawn tradition, we place Gevurah on the right shoulder, not the left. One might expect Gevurah to be in the left shoulder since it's on the left pillar. However, here's where it gets weird. In a temple, the pillars of Severity and Mercy are represented by black and white pilasters that can be moved around the Lodge room. When initiated into the Golden Dawn, the candidate is facing the pillars, while the Hierophant who initiates them is standing between the pillars facing the candidate. So while the candidate is facing East, with the pillar of Severity on the left, the Hierophant is facing West, with the pillar of Severity on their right. When you perform the

> Qabalistic Cross, you are imitating the Hierophant (not the candidate) so the pillar of Severity is on your right. In other words, when you perform the Qabalistic Cross, you are not facing the Tree of Life. Rather, you are in it, facing outwards.

Inhale as you draw your hand back up to your heart. Exhale and intone "ve-Gedulah" (וגדולה) while drawing one arm of the cross of light from your chest into your other shoulder. As before, you may visualize another pillar running through this arm.

Finally, bring both of your hands together in a posture of prayer before your heart or solar plexus and intone "le Olam, Amen" (לעולם אמן). Stand there feeling the presence of the cross and the whole Tree of Life in your body.

Conclusion to the Qabalistic Cross

This practice, while simple, is extraordinarily powerful. It is done at the beginning and end of nearly every Golden Dawn ritual. It aligns your will with the divine will and activates that will as represented in the Tree of Life within the sphere of the magician. Once you can perform this effectively and without notes, you can proceed to the next section.

The Pentagrams

The second section of this ritual is where it gets its name. At this point we will form pentagrams in each of the four directions. Doing this in the banishing form of the ritual (as recommended) is essentially forming four walls to protect your sacred space. (If you are doing it in the invoking form, you are creating four doors. More on that below.)

The Meaning of the Pentagram

The pentagram, or five-pointed star, is one of the oldest and most potent Magickal symbols in the world. It can represent a great many things depending on the context. For example, it can represent the five senses, the human body (two arms, two legs, and a head). It can represent the planet Venus (as her path around the Sun—from the Earth's point-of-view—traces out a five-pointed star). But in our case, it primarily represents the five elements (Earth, Air, Water, Fire, and Spirit) as well as Power, as the number 5 corresponds with Gevurah, the 5th aspect of the divine (or Sephirah) on the Tree of Life.

The Elemental Pentagrams

The Ritual of the Pentagram is an elemental ritual. In its simple (or "lesser") form, it comes in eight varieties: two for each of the four classical or terrestrial elements. That is, Invoking Earth, Banishing Earth, Invoking Air, Banishing Air, *etc*. To begin with, we will only be using the Banishing Earth pentagram, but it's useful to know about all versions and how they work.

Each point of the pentagram corresponds to one of the five elements: that is, the four classical elements plus spirit. The spirit point is at the top, representing the concept of "spirit over matter". (This is why the upright pentagram is considered "good" and the inverted pentagram may be considered "evil" as it places spirit beneath matter, which is the opposite of the spiritual quest.)

The remaining elements are assigned to the pentagram in the following order: Fire-Water-Air-Earth. This corresponds with the elements as laid out in the Tetragrammaton, or four-letter name of God: Yod-Heh-Vav-Heh (יהוה).

The Tetragrammaton and the Elements

There are many names of God in the Hebrew tradition, but one stands apart from them all as the "ineffable" name. "Ineffable" means "cannot be spoken". In Judaism, this name is substituted with "Adonai", another name of God meaning "Lord", or with "Hashem" meaning "the name". In our tradition, we typically spell it out: "Yod-Heh-Vav-Heh". You may have seen this name written out as "Yahweh" (one idea of the proper pronunciation of the name) or "Jehovah" (applying the vowels in "Adonai" to the consonants in "YHVH" or "JHVH" since, in Latin, Y and J are the same letter.). This name is sometimes called the Tetragrammaton, which literally means the four-lettered name of God in Greek. Each of these letters reveals a host of meaning and in sequence, tells the story of creation. First is Yod (י) which, in the Golden Dawn tradition, corresponds with primordial Fire. Think of this as the fire of the big bang exploding the universe into being. Second is Heh (ה), corresponding with the Waters. Note that in the Hebraic tradition, the "Waters" corresponds with what we would today consider the inky blackness of outer space (see Genesis 1:2-7). Third is Vav (ו). This corresponds with the Air that "separates the waters from the waters" (Genesis 1:6) and Qabalistically makes space for the rest of creation. It also reconciles the opposites of the primordial Fire and Water. Finally, the final Heh (ה) represents the Earth in its final form. This also corresponds with manifest reality, while the other three represent a kind of primordial or archetypal essence beyond what we experience in the physical world.

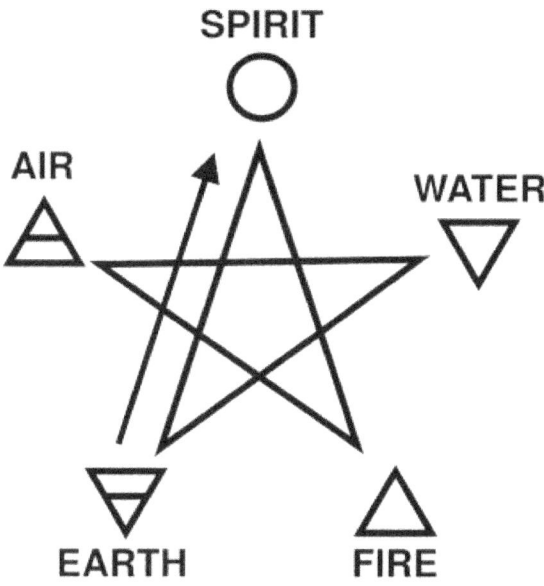

Banishing Pentagram of Earth

The order of the elements placed around the points of the pentagram runs counterclockwise, starting in the lower right corner. The bottom right is Fire, the top right is Water, the top is Spirit, the top left is Air, and the bottom left is Earth. The way each elemental pentagram is traced is going towards the point or away from it for invoking or banishing, respectively. The first thing you'll notice is that there are two ways you could do this, since there are two lines coming out of each point. You always use the upper of the two lines. To banish Earth, you trace from the lower-left corner to the top, or apex. To invoke Air, you trace from the upper right to the upper left. The next thing you'll notice is that means that the invoking pentagram of Air is the same as the banishing pentagram of Water and vice versa. Take this as a lesson in why intention matters and why none of these gestures on their own, without intention, has any Magickal power whatsoever.

The Spirit Pentagrams

To complete this section, I have to say something about the spirit pentagrams. If you've found what I've said about the elemental pentagrams complicated enough, you can happily skip this section and return to it when you learn the Ritual of the Pentagram in its supreme form (see the final chapter on Practical Magick). However, if you've found my explanation incomplete, read on.

So, for the four elements, I said that you always use the upper of the two lines. But what about spirit, where neither line could be considered upper? Well, spirit is the exception. In fact, for spirit, you do not use either of the two lines connected to the apex, but rather the two *lower* lines that you did not use previously. *Two* lower lines, you ask? Yes, two, because the spirit pentagrams come in two flavors: active and passive. The spirit-active pentagram uses the line going from Fire to Air (the two "active" elements) and the spirit-passive pentagram uses the line going from Earth to Water (the two "passive" elements). As before, going towards is invoking and going away is banishing (though I have yet to come across a situation in which one would want to banish the Spiritual element in either form). So going from the lower right to the upper left is in the direction of the apex, and therefore invoking. If you were to go from the upper left, to the lower right, you would be banishing spirit-active.

Usage of the spirit pentagrams is considered "advanced" and not recommended for the beginner. To be clear, it is not because there is anything particularly dangerous about using these pentagrams. It's simply that, without mastering the system up to the point of being ready to use them, you probably won't get very much out of them and will end up wasting your time or, worse, convincing yourself that this stuff doesn't work because you weren't able to make it work for you. It is better to focus on the basics which are, frankly, quite enough for most purposes most of the time.

The Lesser Banishing Ritual of the Pentagram and the Pentagram of Earth

As mentioned, there are 8 forms of the simple or "lesser" ritual of the pentagram. (I dislike the adjective "lesser" as it downplays the significance of this ritual and prefer the term "simple". But historically it has been called the "lesser" ritual, so it is important to know that when you see it discussed elsewhere). Generally speaking, the "lesser" ritual only uses the pentagrams of Earth. This may seem surprising until you remember what I said about the final Heh in the discussion of the Tetragrammaton above: namely that it refers not so much to the element of Earth in the Platonic sense of four elements that compose the material world, but rather to the material world itself (with three other worlds above that). In the spiritual quest, it is often valuable to push away the concerns of the material world which is why we so often perform the Lesser Banishing Ritual of the Pentagram (or LBRP) before we undertake any other endeavor, or often as a practice unto itself for spiritual development and attunement. Thus, among the 12 elemental pentagrams that we have discussed (including the pentagrams for spirit-active and spirit-passive) the banishing pentagram of Earth is the one that, by far, gets the most use.

The God-Names

In erecting the pentagrams in each of the four quarters, we empower them with various names of God. The four God-names that are used in the basic ritual of the pentagram are the Tetragrammaton, described above, Adonai (אדני), Eheieh (אהיה), and AGLA (אגלא). (The Tetragrammaton has already been discussed above.)

אדני – *Adonai*

Adonai (אדני) is one of the more common and well-known names of God. It translates as "Lord" and is the name of God associated with Malkhut. Malkhut is the last and lowest point on the Tree of Life, representing the culmination of creation: the manifest and material world. She is the recipient of divinity and the bride of the creator. While Adonai is a masculine word, it is associated with a feminine energy and is therefore one of the two "passive" names used in this ritual.

> ### On Gender In Qabalistic metaphysics
>
> Binary gender tends to come up a lot, with some forces being denoted "feminine" and others "masculine". The topic of gender is a contentious one in the early 21st century, and it has has become strangely politicized. It can become particularly problematic when other adjectives, like "passive" get associated with gender, like "feminine", which can lead to a mistaken impression that people who are "feminine" (i.e. women) should be "passive." "Feminine" in this context, however, refers to an archetypal quality only loosely connected with the female sex and even more tenuously with human gender. In biological terms, both men and women have both hormones that engender masculine and feminine traits (that is, testosterone and estrogen). Men tend to have a little more testosterone than estrogen and women have the opposite. While these biological differences have psychological, social, and behavioral impact, it is important to understand that as humans, we are both, and have both. No human is 100% masculine nor 100% feminine. Without a mixture of both, you could not survive. It is also true that there are many human qualities associated with "masculine" and "feminine" that are entirely culturally specific. For example, today, in the West, men are often assumed to be better at science and math. Two hundred years ago, the opposite was true: the humanities were considered more "manly" and science was something women studied. In Qabalah, it gets similarly confused. Science and math are associated with the sphere of Hod, which is associated with Mercury (a male god) but sits on the feminine pillar of the Tree of Life. This sort of mixture is common. Given the possibility for confusion in these matters, it's tempting to avoid terms like "masculine" and "feminine" altogether and stick with terms like "active" and "passive", though this wouldn't quite be right, and would also do a

> disservice to the literature. While "feminine" is the more "passive" of the two genders, they are not equivalent. There is an organic quality to gender (or more accurately, sex) that is important here. For example, there are many cases in which the masculine impregnates the feminine. For example, in the Tetragrammaton, the Yod (י) impregnates the Heh (ה) which gives birth to Vav (ו), and so on. Simply referring to the Yod as "active" and Heh as "passive" would fail to capture that connotation.

אהיה - *Eheieh*

If Adonai is the name of God associated with the lowest part of the Tree of Life, Eheieh (אהיה) is associated with the highest part: the Crown. It is short for "Eheieh asher Eheieh" (אהיה אשר אהיה) which is what God said to Moses when Moses asks for a name. Given that Hebrew, like many languages, does not distinguish present from future tense, this phrase can be translated as "I am what I am," "I will be what I will be," or (my favorite), "I am what I will be." The "I am" part of that sentence is "Eheieh" and it is one of the simplest and most transcendent name for God that we have.

As Adonai is one of the "passive" names of God, "Eheieh", along with "YHVH", are both "active" names of God. Since YHVH and Eheieh are placed in the East and West respectively, they form the active axis that runs through the temple when performing the Ritual of the Pentagram.

אגלא - *AGLA*

AGLA (אגלא) is sort of the odd one out. It is not as well-known as the other names. (Similarly, the Archangel associated with the North is not as well-known as the other three. But we'll get to that.) It is a *notariqon*, or Qabalistic acronym, short for "Atah Gibor Le-olam Adonai" (אַתָּה גִּבּוֹר לְעוֹלָם אֲדֹנָי). We've already come across the words "atah" and "le-olam" in the Qabalistic Cross, meaning "thou art" and "forever" respectively. "Adonai", meaning "Lord" has already been discussed. And if you noticed that "Gibor" sounds a bit like "Gevurah", you're not far off.

"Gibur" means mighty. So the whole sentence translates as "Thou, O Lord, art mighty forever." While this name may not be as well-known as the others, it has been used consistently in Ceremonial Magick for at least six hundred years. It is the other of the two "passive" names forming the passive axis between South and North.

4-letter names

Each of these names, in Hebrew, is four letters long: YHVH, ADoNaI, EHeIeH, AGLA. This 4x4 structure establishes a solid base, forming the temple in which to practice Magick: Adonai (אדני), Eheieh (אהיה), and AGLA (אגלא)

```
        י  ה  ו  ה
   א        E        י
   ג                 נ
   ל   N ——┼—— S    ד
   א                 א
              W
        ה  י  ה  א
```

Formulation of the Pentagrams

As before, there is both a gesture component and vocal component to this part of the ritual. There are four steps to the casting of the pentagrams in each of the four quarters.
1. Drawing the Pentagram
2. Sign of the Enterer
3. Sign of Silence
4. Drawing the Circle

Drawing the Pentagram

We have already discussed the twelve pentagrams and how to draw them, but a couple of notes on the physical performance of this are in order. First, regarding the tool: In many Wiccan contexts (and their offshoots) it is traditional to use an athame, or ritual knife, to draw the pentagrams. In the Golden Dawn, you are to use the wand of double power. The wand of double power is the simplest Magickal tool (apart from your own body ... which isn't really simple at all) and the first that a neophyte constructs. It is simply a stick (or dowel) with a white end and a black end. When banishing, you are to hold the black end. When invoking, hold the white end. If you can't get a stick, you can simply use a rolled-up piece of paper and make one side dark with a black pen or pencil.

Or you can always use your finger. I personally like to use two fingers in the "sword" mudra. I sometimes bend my middle finger, so it puts pressure on the nail of my index finger. I find that the tension creates a point of power effective for drawing sigils (like pentagrams) in the air.

Sword Finger/Sword Hand

Sign of the Enterer

Once you draw the pentagram, you empower it with the name. You do this by intoning the name while projecting energy forward using both hands. First, raise your hands to the sides of your head, maybe a couple inches away from your temples. Inhale and project forward, taking a step, lowering your head, and thrusting your hands forward through the center of the pentagram, intoning the God-name for that quarter.

Sign of the Enterer

[from https://sacred-texts.com/oto/lib816.htm]

As you do so, intonate the name of God for that direction: "Yod-Heh-Vav-Heh" for the East, "ADoNaI" for the South, "EHeIeH" for the West, and "AGLA" for the North. You can enhance this further by visualizing each letter projecting outwards as you are intoning them (E - יהוה, S - אדני, W - אהיה, N - אגלא; remember that Hebrew is read from right to left). This can be challenging along with everything else, so don't worry about that at first.

Sign of Silence

Once you have empowered the pentagram by projecting the appropriate name of God into it, you seal the quarter by stepping back and raising your finger to your lips giving the sign of silence, as though you were telling someone to be quiet. This is the sign of Harpocrates.

Drawing the Circle

Once the quarter is fully sealed in this way, raise your arm again, with a wand or dagger or just your finger, and draw a quarter circle to the next cardinal direction—from East to South, for example. Then repeat, drawing the pentagram in that direction, intoning with the sign of the enterer, sealing with the sign of silence, and so on until you've made a complete circle back to the East.

The Archangels

There are four archangels that watch over the work. These archangels are powerful entities that each play many roles in many capacities. It is important to note that while, for the purposes of this ritual, we associate them with the four winds, this in no way limits them. Each of them is a powerful entity that you can (and should) build a relationship with. If you have not worked with any of these archangels before, consider this your introduction to them. If you have, this is a way to strengthen and deepen your relationship with them, and perhaps to learn to work with some new archangels in the process. The four archangels are Raphael (רפאל), Gavriel (or Gabriel – גבריאל), Michael (מיכאל) and Auriel (אוריאל). Archangels are beyond gender. I've often seen each of them rendered with either "he" or "she" pronouns. Some see them all as one gender. Some see the angels associated with the active elements (Air and Fire) as male and those associated with the passive elements (Water and Earth) as female. Some have their own associations based on their own experience. So as not to bias how you see them, I will use "they" below.

רפאל – Raphael

Raphael is the Healer of God (or could also translate as "God has Healed"), and they can be called upon when healing is needed. In the ritual of the pentagram, they are associated with the East Wind, which is hot and moist. As such, we are instructed to visualize them in yellow robes, with purple trim. If you remember your color wheel, you'll note that yellow and purple are opposing, or "flashing" colors.

גבריאל – Gavriel

Gavriel or Gabriel is the messenger of God. In fact, all angels are messengers of God, but Gavriel is perhaps most well-known for this function. They are the one that delivered the Qur'an to Mohammed, for example. In the ritual of the pentagram, they are associated with the West Wind, which is cold and moist, like an ocean spray. As such, we are instructed to visualize them in blue robes with yellow trim. As with Raphael, these are opposing, or "flashing" colors.

מיכאל – Michael

Michael is the warrior of God, often depicted defeating Satan in Christian iconography. They are a protector and deliverer of justice and can help when that is needed. In the ritual of the pentagram, they are associated with the South Wind, which is hot and dry, like a desert wind. We are instructed to visualize them in red robes with green trim, also flashing colors.

אוריאל – Auriel

Auriel or Uriel is the Light of God. Less well known than the other three, this archangel is associated with the North Wind, which is cold and dry. Unlike the other three archangels, this one is to be visualized with the colors: russet, citrine, olive, and black, the four colors associated with Malkhut. These are all dark, earthy colors. Russet has the look of red clay. Citrine is a sort of dark yellow color. Olive looks like a green olive. And black, of course, is black.

Evocation of the Archangels

Once the pentagrams have been formed, the magician returns to the center of the circle and faces East once again. Holding their arms out in the form of a cross, the recite:

Before me, RAPHAEL (רפאל)
Behind me, GAVRIEL (גבריאל)
At my right hand, MICHAEL (מיכאל)
At my left hand, AURIEL (אוריאל)
For about me flame the pentagrams
And within me shines the six-rayed star.

...vibrating each of the names.

The archangels and pentagrams have now been explained, but the six-rayed star is new. It is generated implicitly as a result of the ceremony. The six-rayed star will be explained in more detail in the chapter on the ritual of the hexagram, below. But for now, suffice it to say that the hexagram, and the cross, both symbolize the union of opposites. In the hexagram, it is a little more obvious in that you have an upward facing triangle coming to meet a downward facing triangle. These two triangles can mean a number of things, including water ∇ and fire Δ, feminine and masculine, or, in this case, your will (directed upward) and the divine will (directed downward) coming to meet each other in your heart.

Conclusion

After evoking the four archangels, we perform the Qabalistic Cross once again. Here is the entire ceremony in summary:

1. Qabalistic Cross
    a. "Atah" (thou art...) [draw down light to head]
    b. "Malkhut" (the Kingdom) [draw down to belly]
    c. "ve Gevurah" (and the Power) [touch right shoulder]
    d. "ve Gedulah" (and the Glory) [touch left shoulder]
    e. "le olam Amen" (forever, Amen) [hands at heart]
2. Ward the Quarters with Banishing Pentagrams
    a. Draw Pentagram and Vibrate "Yod-Heh-Vav-Heh" (or "YeHoVaH" or "IAO")
    b. Draw Pentagram and Vibrate "Ah-doh-nye" in the South
    c. Draw Pentagram and Vibrate "Eh-heh-yeh" in the West
    d. Draw Pentagram and Vibrate "Ah-Ge-Lah." in the North
3. Invoke Guardians
    a. "Before me, RAPHAEL"
    b. "Behind me, GAVRIEL" (or "GABRIEL")
    c. "At my right hand, MICHAEL"
    d. "At my left hand, AURIEL" (or "URIEL")
    e. "For about me flame the pentagrams; and within me shines the six-rayed star."
4. Qabalistic Cross (again)

This ritual should become your daily practice for at least a week until it can be performed completely and easily from memory, even better if done twice daily. Begin with just the Qabalistic Cross and practice until you can do it fluidly and feel the power of it within you. Then add the formulation of the pentagrams and the evocation of the archangels. Do not rush it, but do not delay, either. Performing the ritual, even if you have to read the book while doing so, or making mistakes, is better than not doing it at all. The ritual can be done very quickly, though I recommend you take your time with it if you are able. But again, doing it quickly is better than not doing it at all. Finally, you can always do it in your imagination. It is better to do it physically, with both gestures and words. But if you cannot, again, better to do it in your imagination (or with just words or just gestures) than not at all.

Middle Pillar

In the original Order of the Golden Dawn in the Outer, the Lesser Banishing Ritual of the Pentagram was the only ritual that was taught to the Neophyte. Then, in 1936, Israel Regardie wrote *The Middle Pillar* which argued that this ritual, traditionally reserved for Adepts of the Order, was too important, too valuable, to be reserved only for such a limited audience. Since then, the Middle Pillar has been added to the basic instruction in most Golden Dawn-style Orders.

It is, in some ways, not unlike the practice in Yoga of activating the chakras from the root to the crown. However, it is different in (at least) two significant ways. First, and most obvious, is that it uses *sephirot* of the Middle Pillar of the Qabalistic Tree of Life, and not the Yogic Chakras. Second, and more subtle, is that it goes from the top down, and not the bottom up. This difference gives it a distinctly different feel.

I have done both practices and recommend both. They are different. I do not recommend doing both together, as that is more likely to cause confusion. People have tried to equate the *sephirot* with the chakras, but I do not recommend this either. It is tempting to do so, since both consist of seven vertical levels. And there are some points where the two are extremely similar. For example, both *Yesod* (sephirah) and *Svadhisthana* (chakra) are associated with the genital region, both associated with the Moon, and so forth. *Tipharet* and *Anahata* are both located in the heart and carry many of the associations you would expect for that. But they also differ in some significant ways. For example, *Tipharet* is associated with the quintessence, spirit, while *Anahata* is associated with the element of water.

Ten Sephirot

The *Sepher Yetzirah* tells us that there are ten *sephirot* (singular: *sephirah*). But what is a *sephirah*? It doesn't exactly tell us. In the last chapter, I talked about "aspects of the divine". This is probably the purest definition of *sephirah* you will find, but it is not entirely satisfying. I've seen the word "sphere" used sometimes in place of *sephirah* which is convenient because it has a similar sound and because *sephirot* are traditionally depicted as circles in diagrams of the Tree of Life.

The Qabalah teaches us that the ten *sephirot* are attributes of God and that they relate to each other in a gradual unfolding. That is, they are sequential, but they are not entirely linear. The sequence oscillates between three pillars, the Pillar of Mercy, the Pillar of Severity, and the Middle Pillar between them. They can be described from the top down, or from the bottom up. Since the bottom is closest to our everyday experience, we will start there.

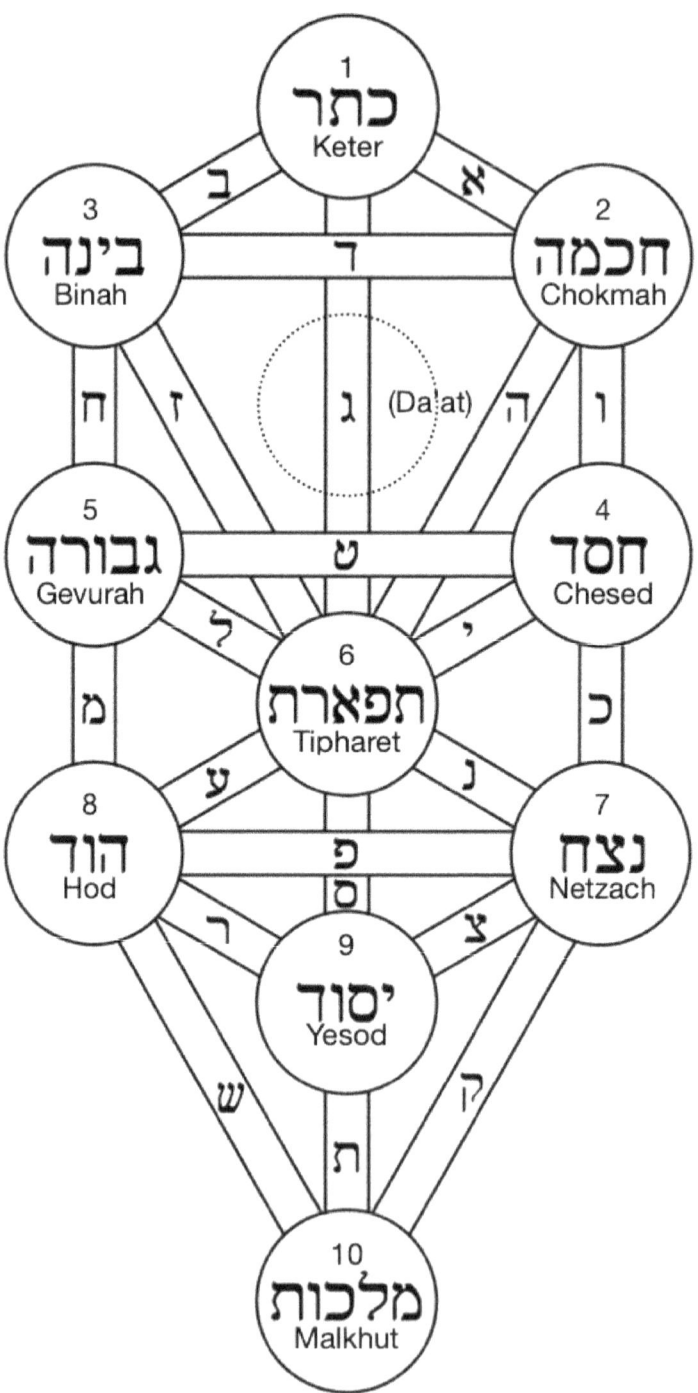

The Qabalistic Tree

10 - Malkhut (or Malkuth)

Malkhut (מלכות) literally means Kingdom. In its lowest form, it represents the material world. One of the teachings of Qabalah (and most mystical systems that I'm aware of) is that God is both transcendent and immanent. That means that God is both "out there" and "right here". This is a paradox, but paradox is quite common when talking about something that surpasses human comprehension (like the divine). Traditional religion tends to talk about God as "out there", someone far away, like a king on a mountaintop, or in the clouds. In a sense, this is true, at least when speaking from the point of view of ordinary consciousness.

But when you enter a mystical state of consciousness, God moves from "nowhere" to "now here". Though Malkhut is considered the "furthest" from the Crown in terms of the geometry of the Tree of Life, it is nonetheless an aspect of God that is right here with us, right now, if only we were to see it. But since that is not so easy, we are forced to look upward. The name of God associated with Malkhut is *Adonai ha-Aretz* (Lord of the Earth) or simply *Adonai* (אדני).

9 - Yesod

Yesod (יסוד) means Foundation. It is the sephirah closest to Malkhut, but one step away, one step above. It is sometimes considered "the engine room" of reality. As it is a little bit abstracted from the material world, I like to think of it as the domain of the mathematical laws that govern the universe. It is the realm of ideas, the blueprints of reality, if you will. As it is the closest sephirah to the Earth, it is also associated with the Moon. It is likewise associated with the unconscious. The names of God associated with Yesod are *El Chai* (אל חי)—Living God) or *El Shaddai* (אל שדי—God Almighty) or *Shaddai El Chai* (שדי אל חי—Almighty Living God).

8 & 7 - Hod and Netzach

Above Yesod are two sephirot, one on the left (Hod) and one on the right (Netzach). Hod (הוד) means "Splendor" and Netzach (נצח) means "Victory". They are the two lowest points on the left and right pillars of Severity and Mercy, respectively. At the risk of being overly simplistic, we can associate them with functions commonly associated with the left and right hemispheres of the brain, respectively. So, for example, as the left hemisphere is responsible for language and so-called "linear" thinking, so is Hod. As the right hemisphere is responsible for "holistic" thinking, so is Netzach. They are associated with the two inner planets, Mercury and Venus, respectively. The names of God associated with them are Elohim Tzabaot (צבאות אלהים) for Hod and YHVH Tzabaot (יהוה צבאות) for Netzach.

6 - Tipharet (or Tiphareth)

Tipharet (תפארת) is the heart of the Tree of Life, halfway between Keter (the Crown) and Malkhut (the Kingdom), between the Pillar of Mercy and the Pillar of Severity. It translates as Beauty, indicating the harmony that comes in the reconciliation of opposites. It is associated with the Sun and the heart of the human body. The name of God associated with Tipharet is "YHVH Eloah ve-Da'at" (יהוה אלוה ודעת). "YHVH" being the Tetragrammaton described in the last chapter. "Eloah ve-Da'at" meaning, "God of Knowledge". The Tetragrammaton itself is also associated with this sephirah.

5 & 4 - Gevurah (or Geburah) and Chesed

Above Tipharet, but below the supernal triad, are Gevurah (גבורה) and Chesed (חסד). We discussed these sephirot in the Qabalistic Cross. There, Chesed was called Gedulah (Glory), another name for Chesed. Gevurah represents power, or strength, and sits in the middle of the pillar of severity. Chesed means mercy, and sits in the middle of the pillar of the same. Either, without balance, is evil. "Unbalanced Mercy is weakness and the fading out of the Will. Unbalanced Severity is cruelty and the barrenness of Mind."[2] The two opposites resolve themselves in Tipharet. Gevurah corresponds with the planet Mars. Chesed corresponds with the planet Jupiter. The names of God associated with these two sephirot are Elohim Gibor (אלהים גבור) for Gevurah and El (אל) for Chesed.

Da'at (or Daath) and the Abyss

There is a separation between the lower seven sephirot and the upper three—often referred to as the supernal triad. That separation is sometimes called the Abyss to represent the fact that there is no way for the *ego* (or "I") to cross it. Above the abyss, opposites collapse into one another, the distinction between good and evil ceases to exist.

In this space between the supernal triad and the lower seven sephirot is a kind of pseudo-sephirah called Da'at (דעת), which means "Knowledge". In one sense, it is the logical outcome of Wisdom and Understanding (Chokmah and Binah) and you'll notice it is part of the name of God associated with Tipharet. On the way down, Wisdom distills into Understanding which forms the basis of Knowledge. But on the way up, Knowledge can also be a barrier because when you think you know something, it can become impossible to go any further, blocking you from true understanding (let alone wisdom). This is why the Zen master Shunryu Suzuki urged his students to maintain the "beginner's mind".

Since Da'at is not a proper sephirot, it does not have a name of God associated with it. However, for the purposes of the Middle Pillar exercise, it utilizes the name associated with Binah, which is "YHVH Elohim" or simply "Elohim".

---

[2] Lecture of the Hierophant in the Neophyte Ritual, from pg 125 of *the Golden Dawn* by Israel Regardie, 6th Ed.

3 & 2 - Binah and Chokmah

Above the Abyss but below the Crown are Binah (בינה) and Chokmah (חכמה), or Understanding and Wisdom. Like Hod and Netzach, these can be associated with the left and right hemispheres of the brain respectively, only on a higher order. The left hemisphere is responsible for producing language, without which there can be no Understanding. The right hemisphere is without the ability to articulate language, but because of its capacity for holistic understanding it is associated with Chokmah, or the Wisdom that is beyond language. Binah is associated with the outermost of the classical planets, Saturn. Binah also sits at the top of the Pillar of Severity while Chokmah sits atop the Pillar of Mercy. The names of God associated with these two Sephirot are YHVH Elohim (יהוה אלהים) for Binah and Yah (יה) for Chokmah.

1 - Keter (or Kether)

Above even wisdom is pure will, or causality. This is the Crown, or Keter (כתר), of the Tree of Life. It is difficult to say anything about this sephirah, which is why the name of God associated with Keter is simply "Eheieh asher Eheieh" or "I am that I am", or simply "Eheieh" (אהיה).

> ### WHAT ABOUT THE QLIPPOT?
>
> In recent years there's been more interest in the Qlippot (or Qlippoth). While the Tree of Life already has a light, right-hand path (including Netzach, Chesed, and Chokmah) and a dark, left-hand path (including Hod, Gevurah, and Binah), there are those who like their spirituality darker than dark, and so are understandably attracted to this inverted Tree of Life. In many ways it is symbolically similar to the inverted pentagram which places spirit below matter. The Qlippot are the broken vessels of the Tree of Life. The idea is that when the light first came down into the vessels of the sephirot, the vessels could not contain the light and so they shattered. These shattered pieces fell and now sit below Malkhut as a kind of inverted Tree of Life. It is here

that unclean and unredeemed spirits come from. They are largely seen as distortions of sephirot of the Tree of Life, so each sephirah has it Qlippotic equivalent. Gevurah, being the sephirah most associated with the pillar of severity, is considered "closest" to its Qlippotic counterpart in that it is very easy to flip over into the evil version of that sephirah. You can see this in the human world when the police, a force that is supposed to protect us from violence, becomes corrupt and a source of violence in itself. I do not recommend working with the Qlippot directly; I find the Tree of Life has enough dimensionality in itself. One need not invoke corruption in order to work with the dark forces of war (Mars, Gevurah) and death (Saturn, Binah). That said, one of the things that Qabbalah teaches us is that, at a certain point, all things resolve into their opposites, and above the Abyss, there is no distinction between good and evil. So it is at least theoretically possible to reach the same point by going downwards instead of upwards, but again, not recommended.

Practice

The Middle Pillar is most often done after the Lesser Ritual of the Pentagram. It consists of intoning, or vibrating, the Godnames of each of the sephirot along the middle pillar of the Tree of Life, including Da'at (borrowing the name from Binah). This Middle Pillar runs down the central channel of the body with Keter (appropriately) at the crown of the head, Da'at at the throat, Tipharet at the heart, Yesod at the genitals, and Malkhut at the feet. The placement of each sephirah at each point of the body is more than incidental. Keter, placed at the crown of the head, represents that which is beyond thought. Da'at, placed in the throat, represents the knowledge articulated through speech. Tipharet, at the heart, represents both balance (being at the center of the body) and wise compassion. Yesod, at the genitals, represents generation itself. Malkhut, at the feet, represents establishment and groundedness in the material world.

This exercise is typically done standing. It can be done sitting, or even lying down if necessary. But the preferred posture is standing if possible. Sitting upright is second-best. Lying down is less effective because the association with the sephirot being stacked vertically from earth to heaven is lost, but it can still be done that way if needed (for example, if you are sick or otherwise incapable of getting up, and need to strengthen your etheric body).

Descent of the Light

Begin with the Crown and intone (vibrate) "Eheieh Asher Eheieh" or simply "Eheieh" at least three or four times, visualizing brilliant white light at the crown of your head. If you cannot vocalize the God-name, do so deliberately and slowly in your imagination, hearing the sound as clearly as you can. Whispering or subvocalizing is better than nothing. But the important thing is to engage your consciousness fully with the sounds of this name and the light at the crown of your head.

Inhale and exhale, drawing the light down into your throat. Don't rush it. If you want to take more than one breath to do this, and get settled into your throat, do so. Once there, visualize the light expanding in your throat as a blue-gray sphere. There, intone "Yod-Heh-Vav-Heh Elohim" or simply "Elohim" at least three or four times.

Inhale and exhale, drawing the light down into the center of your chest. As before, go slowly. Once there, visualize the light expanding as a radiant golden sphere, like the sun. There intone "Yod-Heh-Vav-Heh Eloah ve-Da'at" or simply "Yod-Heh-Vav-Heh", at least three or four times.

Inhale and exhale, drawing the light down to your genitals. There, visualize the light as in a radiant violet sphere. Intone the name "Shaddai El-Chai" at least three or four times.

Finally, inhale and exhale, drawing the light down into your feet. There, visualize it in olive green. Intone the name "Adonai Ha-Aretz" or simply "Adonai" at least three or four times.

Circulating the Light

Once you are able to perform the Descent of the Light easily and without reference to notes, you should follow this practice by circulating the light. There are three ways to circulate the light. You can do it in one, two, or all three ways. In each case, you inhale up, and exhale down.

1. You may circulate the light by going up the back of your spine and down the front of your chest. This follows the path of sensory signals going up the back of the spinal cord and motor signals going down the front.
2. You may circulate the light going up along the column of severity (the side where you place Gevurah in the Qabalistic Cross) and down the column of mercy (the side where you place Gedulah).
3. You may circulate the light going up the center, and out like a shower around you.

Repeat at least three times before moving on to the next.

Ritual of the Hexagram

As stated before, in the original Order of the Golden Dawn, only the Ritual of the Pentagram was taught. While the Middle Pillar was reserved for the Adepts of the Inner Order, there is no reason that I can see why it is not perfectly appropriate for the Neophyte to practice along with the Ritual of the Pentagram.

The Ritual of the Hexagram is a bit different. While the Ritual of the Pentagram lifts the magician from Malkhut to Yesod, the work of the Ritual of the Hexagram is squarely in Tipharet. It invokes the dying God formula: INRI and IAO. The most well-known exemplar of the dying God is the Christ, Jesus, but he is not the only one, and from a Hermetic perspective, not even the most important. The most important is the Egyptian god, Osiris.

Analysis of the Keyword(s)

Isis, Apophis, Osiris

Osiris and his sister/wife Isis (gods don't seem to worry much about incest) were two of the principal deities in the Egyptian pantheon. Osiris is the reason the sun is reborn each day. In this early and prototypical myth of the dying god, Osiris is killed and dismembered by his vengeful brother Set, or Apophis. His wife, Isis, puts him back together again.

> ### EGYPTIAN VS. HEBREW
> One of the things that I found most surprising, even disturbing, when first approaching the system of the Golden Dawn was the interplay between Egyptian and Hebrew symbolism. If you've ever been to a Jewish Passover Seder, you'll know that in Judaism, "Egypt" is considered a symbol of bondage, slavery, and everything a liberated person is trying to get away from. This comes from the second book of the Torah:

Exodus, in which Moses led the Hebrews from slavery in Egypt to "the Promised Land". This Bible story is probably the most well-known and repeated, outside of the story of Jesus. It was at the center of the civil rights movement in the 20th century. So, when I first encountered this mixture of Hebrew Qabalah with Egyptian gods, it seemed terribly incongruent to me. But in time, I realized that the image of Egypt in the Passover story is extremely limited and incomplete. For one thing, in esoteric lore, it has long been thought that Moses learned Egyptian Magick while living as the adopted grandson of the Pharaoh. Furthermore, the whole reason the Hebrews were in Egypt was because they had found a good home there ... for a while. Finally, it's worth noting that the Hermetic tradition is not Jewish, nor is it Egyptian. It is syncretic, which means it's a mixture of many traditions, from Greek, Egyptian, Jewish, Christian, even incorporating Arabic and Indian elements, not to mention English, and so on. In an age of orthodox religion and fundamentalist preachers, the very concept of syncretism can seem unnatural—but most of the world, for most of history, has been syncretic. In fact, so far as I know, until recently, the only religions that considered themselves mutually exclusive with other religions are the ones descended from Moses, that is: Judaism, Christianity, and Islam. For most of history, in most of the world, religions happily intermingled. Buddhist temples in Japan often have Shinto shrines on the grounds and vice versa. The Buddha is honored as a Hindu god and Hindu gods play a role in Buddhism. In China, people borrow from Daoism, Confucianism, Buddhism, and other religious philosophies as the occasion requires. And in the ancient Near East, where Hermeticism came into existence, magicians drew upon Egyptian, Hebraic, Arabic, and other forms in order to work their Magick as well.

Cycle of Nature

The cycle of life, death, rebirth can be seen in the cycle of nature, such as the seasons of the year and even the course of the day. The sun is reborn each morning, and each year. If you've ever wondered why

Christmas is on December 25th, it's because it's the first day after the Winter Solstice in which the sun is visibly seen to rise earlier in the morning. For the last six months, the days have gotten shorter and shorter, and it could seem as though the sun was fading away into eternal darkness. But on December 25th, a few days after the darkest day, and longest night of the year, the sun rises a bit earlier, and there is a bit more sunlight than the day before. In the pagan Roman calendar, this was the day of Solis Invicti, the unconquerable sun. The early Christian church put the birthday of their god on the same day to capitalize on the similarities between the two deities and the enthusiasm already felt for the return of the sun/Son.

Keywords

There are three keywords analyzed in the Ritual of the Hexagram and they are all alike, but also different. They are, INRI, IAO, and LVX.

I.N.R.I.

Christians (and those with a Christian education) will recognize I.N.R.I. as the acronym placed over the cross on which Jesus was crucified. The traditional interpretation is that the crime of the crucified was written at the top of the cross. In Jesus' case, it said that he was "*Iēsus Nazarēnus, Rēx Iūdaeōrum*" or Jesus the Nazarene, King of the Jews. Later, Rosicrucians found other interpretations for this four-letter acronym, including "*Intra Nobis Regnum Iehova,*" meaning "The Kingdom of God is within us" and "*Igne Natura Renovatur Integra,*" meaning "Nature is completely renewed by fire".

In the Golden Dawn tradition, these Roman letters are transcribed into the Hebrew: Yod-Nun-Resh-Yod along with their Qabalistic significance. Yod (י) represents Virgo, which corresponds with the mighty mother goddess Isis. Nun (נ) represents Scorpio, which corresponds with Set or Apophis the destroyer. Resh (ר) represents the Sun, which corresponds with Osiris, who was slain and rose again.

I.A.O.

IAO is a Gnostic name for God, equivalent to the Tetragrammaton. (It may even be a proper pronunciation of the Tetragrammaton.) In Roman letters, it is also an acronym for Isis, Apophis, and Osiris. (This is why we use the name Apophis instead of Set throughout this ritual.)

IAO is a powerful vibratory formula. In fact, it can be used as an alternative to the God-names used in the Middle Pillar by breaking it apart into five vowel sounds: I, E, A, O, U, and vibrating each vowel sound with each of the sephirot (**I** for Keter, **E** for Da'at, **A** for Tipharet, **O** for Yesod, and **U** for Malkhut).

> There is something called the I.A.O. formula that describes the growth experience. Students of learning will recognize this pattern, though under different names. First comes the Isis phase. This is the phase associated with "beginner's luck". Everything seems to go easy. Things are exciting and fresh and new. It is as though the mother goddess herself were shepherding you along. Then something happens. Beginner's luck runs out. The goddess vanishes. Everything gets hard. You've entered the Apophis stage. This is the stage where most people give up. You will likely experience this yourself (if you haven't already) in your pursuit of Magick. Perhaps you've experienced it more than once. If you stick with it though, something shifts. Things get easier, but in a different way. You're now operating on a new level, with a certain degree of mastery. Some part of you has been "reborn" in a sense, like Osiris.

L.V.X.

LVX is the last of the three words used in this ritual. In Latin, it means Light, as in "Fiat Lvx" meaning "let there be light", the first words uttered by God in the Biblical story of Creation. Light is a symbol of knowledge, understanding, wisdom, and the divine itself.

Like the two before it, the letters correspond with the gods Isis, Apophis, and Osiris, but this time in terms of their shape. Holding your arms in the shape of an 'L' represents the mourning of Isis when her brother/husband was slain. Holding your arms up, in the shape of a 'V' represents Apophis, triumphant over his brother Osiris. Holding your arms crossed over your chest in the shape of an 'X' represents Osiris, slain and risen.

Performance

After performing the lesser banishing Ritual of the Pentagram, begin by intoning "I.N.R.I." Then, with a wand or your finger, trace the Hebrew letters, and intone them while doing so: "Yod, Nun, Resh, Yod".

Then extend your arms in the form of a cross and say, "The sign of Osiris slain." Raise your right arm up, making the sign of "L" and say "The sign of the mourning of Isis." Then raise both arms above your head in the shape of a "V" and say, "The sign of Typhon, Apophis." Then cross your arms over your chest in an "X" and say, "The sign of Osiris risen."

Then repeat the gestures, saying, "L," "V," "X," as you do so. Then, with your arms still crossed over your chest, vibrate "LUX" loudly, filling the room with the Latin word for light.

Next, put your arms out to your side, making a T and say "The light," and bring your arms back together in the shape of an X and say "...of the cross." Then recite the following:

Virgo, Isis, Mighty Mother
Scorpio, Apophis, Destroyer
Sol, Osiris, Slain and Risen
Isis, Apophis, Osiris

Then vibrate, "IAO" slowly and with great volume, gradually raising your arms out to your side, filling the room with sacred sound. Finally, slowly lower your hands and arms, out to your side, and say, "let the divine light descend," feeling the room fill with light.

> **LATIN AND GREEK**
>
> We've already discussed Hebrew as a Magickal language, and arguably the two most important in the Western world. (Sanskrit would be the Eastern equivalent of Hebrew, with an astonishing level of similarity in terms of how they are discussed in their respective literature.) Two other languages that come up often, secondary to Hebrew, but also important, are Latin and ancient Greek. LVX and INRI are Latin. IAO is Greek. Though these languages don't have the mythological status of Hebrew, through millennia of repeated use in religious and Magickal contexts, they have taken on a great degree of spiritual power in the European (and, by extension, American) consciousness.
>
> As an aside, among the Magickal languages discussed in this book, Hebrew is the only one that is once again in popular usage. Latin has its descendants in Italian, Spanish, and so on, but is otherwise used only for religious and Magickal purposes. (Since Vatican II, even the religious uses have waned, leaving it almost entirely in the hands of Magicians and scholars.) Ancient Greek has modern Greek as its descendant, but the two languages are, again, quite different, and Ancient Greek today is used almost entirely for religious and Magickal purposes. Hebrew was in a similar status as these until the mid-20th century, at which point it became the national language of the state of Israel and once again entered popular usage. This in no way diminishes its Magickal power, though I do find it interesting from a Magickal-historical point of view. There are many who believe that we have entered a new age, whether it's the age of Aquarius or the æon of Horus. It's hard not to see the re-emergence of Hebrew as a spoken language as somehow connected to this.

The Hexagrams

As with the pentagrams, described in the Ritual of the Pentagram, there are a great number of hexagrams—20, in fact, not counting the hexagrams for the Sun. There are two for each of the classical planets, and two for each of the cardinal elements. In this case, the elements have

Planetary Hexagrams

The planetary hexagrams are not used in the simple ritual of the hexagram but are still worth knowing. Like the pentagrams, their association is based upon the points. Unlike the pentagrams, the difference between invoking and banishing has to do with whether you are going clockwise or anti-clockwise (as opposed to towards or away-from, in the case of the pentagrams). The arrangement of the planets is as they are on the Tree of Life with Saturn (normally associated with Binah) displaced to Da'at (in a pattern we've already seen in the Middle Pillar exercise). So that means that the Moon (☽) is at the bottom (with Yesod), Mercury (☿) is in the lower left (with Hod), Venus (♀) is in the lower right (with Netzach), the Sun is in the middle (with Tipharet), Mars (♂) is in the upper left (with Gevurah), Jupiter (♃) is in the upper right (with Chesed) and Saturn (♄) is at the top (with Da'at). For each of the hexagrams, excepting the Sun, you start with the point associated with that planet and trace clockwise if invoking, and anti-clockwise if banishing. You then do the opposite triangle in the same direction. So, for example, if you're invoking the Moon, you'd begin at the bottom, go up to the upper-left, across to the upper right, then back to the bottom, then start at the top, go clockwise to the lower right, across to the lower left, then back to the top. You would then trace the symbol of the moon in the center of the hexagram. For the Sun, you do all of the hexagrams.

The Planets

The seven classical planets have been used in Magickal systems throughout the world. It is difficult to know exactly how the associations between the physical planets and their divine counterparts came to be, but they are spread throughout the ancient world with a remarkable degree of consistency. That said, the planets, and the gods associated with them, are not so cut-and-dried like the elements. Still, they form a remarkably useful way of categorizing phenomena and working with powers: complex enough to be nuanced, but simple enough to be fairly easily apprehended.

The planets are so ancient that they predate our understanding of a heliocentric solar system. In some texts they were referred to as the "wandering stars" because, unlike other stars, their movement "wanders" to and fro, while the "fixed stars" or stationary stars (that is, actual stars) rotate around the Earth (from the Earth's point of view).

The two "planets" that are not planets at all are our Sun and our Moon. Qabalistically, these correspond with Tipharet and Yesod, respectively. The Sun is at the heart of the Tree of Life just as it is the heart of our solar system. The Moon reflects that light as Yesod reflects the light of Tipharet down to Earth/Malkhut.

The Moon

Just as the Earth orbits the Sun in an approximately 365-day cycle (*i.e.* one solar year), the Moon orbits the Earth in an approximately 28 day cycle (*i.e.* one lunar month). Our calendar months are a bit longer in order to make 12 months fit into one solar year. Just as the Earth, on its course around the Sun, goes through the seasons of the year; the Moon, on its course around the Earth, goes through its stations. The Moon waxes (gets bigger) and wanes (gets smaller). It can be new, crescent, half, gibbous, or full.

> HALF-MOON
>
> One point of confusion to watch out for: a "half-moon" can refer either to a moon that is half full (that is, one quarter of its way through its cycle) or halfway through its cycle (that is, full). The former is more common, but you may see the latter sometimes, so it's worth pointing out. In that case, a "quarter

> moon" would be what we would normally refer to as a "waxing half-moon" since that is a quarter of the way through the cycle.

The Moon is sometimes cited as the best evidence of how the heavenly bodies affect us. While no heavenly body comes close to affecting us as much as the Sun (whose influence is so great it is difficult to even conceive of life without it), the Moon does affect us in interesting and subtle ways. It is close enough to our Earth, and big enough, that its presence pulls upon the waters of the Earth, creating the tides. If not for tides, life would most likely never have developed on Earth. There are those who believe in "lunacy", the tendency for people to act a little "crazy" during the full Moon. While this has been shown not to be true, the association between the moon and madness remains in the imagination. And of course, there are menstrual cycles which may follow a lunar cycle (though rarely accurately).

It is for these reasons that the Moon is associated with the waters of the unconscious. Just as most of the Earth is underwater and therefore invisible to us, most of the psyche is unconscious. So just as the Moon interacts with the ocean, so is its spiritual component said to interact with the human unconscious. It therefore rules over dreams, instincts, and other elements of our being that are below the threshold of consciousness, and that are often "primitive". Qabalistically, the color associated with Yesod and the Moon is Purple.

Mercury & Venus

Between the Earth and the Sun are Mercury and Venus. These correspond with the Sephirot of Hod and Netzach on the pillars of Severity and Mercy, respectively. They are the lowest emanations of duality and Qabalistically correspond with the left and right hemispheres of the brain. Mercury is Hermes in Greek, and Venus is Aphrodite. Put the two together and you have the alchemical Hermaphrodite. The term "hermaphrodite" is an archaic term for *intersex*, that is, someone with both male and female primary and/or secondary sex characteristics. The concept comes from a mystical union of the two sides of ourselves, often represented as the male and female. In Hinduism, this same concept appears in Ardhanarishvara, who is a combination of Shiva and Parvati and is depicted in much the same way: male on one half, female on the other.

It is interesting to note that the masculine in this case is Mercury, not Mars, the god more commonly associated with masculinity. (The symbol for man being the one for Mars: ♂, while the one for woman being for Venus: ♀.) The violence of Mars is balanced by the generosity of Jupiter. Ironically, it is both Mars and Mercury that are associated with the "feminine" pillar of Severity. You'll recall I alluded to this in the section on Gender in the Ritual of the Pentagram.

Mercury

Mercury is the messenger of the gods. First and foremost, he is the god of communication. He is associated not only with Hermes, but with the Egyptian god Thoth. Being the god of communication, he is also the god of writing, Magick, science, grammar, mathematics, education, and so on. He is a good god to talk to when you need help communicating, taking a test, or anything that would involve verbal or written communication. Qabalistically, the color associated with Hod and Mercury is Orange.

Venus

Venus is the goddess of love and sex. She is Aphrodite in the Greek pantheon. She represents that which (non-verbally) connects people to one another, and she also has a particular connection to the Earth. It is, perhaps, a poor comment on the ancient conception of the planets, but of the planets, she is the one that is particularly "feminine". (The Moon is often also considered feminine, though not archetypally so, like Venus.) Qabalistically, the color associated with Netzach and Venus is Green.

The Sun

The Sun is the center of our solar system and the source of all life. In ancient times it was identified with the Creator and in a way, that wasn't far off. Today we understand that though the universe existed before there was a Sun, if not for our Sun, there would be no life on Earth. So, from our terrestrial point of view, the Sun really is our "Father in Heaven" who impregnated our Mother Earth with the seed of Life.

Note that many father gods are associated with Jupiter, not the Sun, and we will get into that below. In fact, since we now know that the Sun is not the source of creation, we can look beyond the Sun for that source which makes the Sun the Son of that source, as in the Son of God in the Christian tradition. Christ, Osiris, and all the dying and resurrected solar deities for whom we traditionally celebrate their birth in the days following the Winter Solstice when the days are beginning to get longer again (*i.e.* Christmas), are the gods associated with the Sun. Qabalistically, the Sun is where we meet our own personal guardian angel who, like the Christ, is a mediator between our own small selves and the infinite beyond. This Christ-self then becomes our own inner Self, once divested of all the dross that keeps us distracted from the divine. The goal of High Magick is to realize this "higher" Self, hence the term self-realization: the making real of the Self. The color of Tipharet and the Sun is Yellow, like gold.

Mars

Mars is the god of war. He is associated with Gevurah, the sephirah of Power, in the center of the pillar of Severity. Of all the sephirot, this is the one where it is most easy to flip into its qlippotic equivalent, for power can be intoxicating, severity becomes cruelty, and the desire for justice can morph into vengeance. That said, without engaging with Mars and directing his Power, we ourselves would be weak. Our passivity would become the accomplice of evil by allowing it to thrive. Thus, we must engage with this power, but be very careful when doing so. This is, perhaps, the most difficult task, and one that is fitting to be taken up *after* the self-realization that comes with Knowledge and Conversation with your Holy Guardian Angel in the Sun. (See the chapter on Knowledge and Conversation in Part II.) This is why it is beyond the Sun in the Tree of Life. From a heliocentric perspective, it is also the first planet that has us moving *away* from the Sun. Just as Mars is "the red planet" owing to its red hue, the color of Mars and Gevurah is red. One should be careful when working with Mars as it can lead to rage.

Jupiter

Qabalistically, Jupiter represents the beneficent Father. The archetype of "Father" is a complicated one, and for many, "beneficent" might not be the first word that comes to mind when they think of their father. Jupiter is also not always the most beneficent god in the Roman pantheon. But in his role corresponding with Chesed on the Tree of Life, we should think of him that way. If "Father" doesn't work for you, perhaps "Santa Claus" gets closer to the image we're going for here, only in this case, the color we'll use is cool blue. If Mars and Gevurah are rage and severity, then Jupiter and Chesed are kindness and mercy. Jupiter, in this context, is generous. If you want wealth, Jupiter is the god you want to go to.

Saturn

Saturn is death. Saturn is a quiet heaviness. Saturn is the one and only planet that lies beyond the Abyss on the Tree of Life. Saturn is associated with Binah or Wisdom, for it is by facing death that we attain a deeper wisdom. Saturn is both the most distant planet, but in a subtle way, is also the most intimate. Death is always near us, within us, and under our feet. When living beings die, they return to the Earth. Death is our constant companion, and yet one that can be difficult to see. This is why Saturn, while on the one hand corresponding to the sephirot beyond the Abyss, also corresponds with the last letter of the Hebrew aleph-bet, Tav (ת), which is the first path we must cross when ascending the Tree of Life (see the section on Pathworking in Part II). One should be careful when working with Saturn as it can lead to depression.

Elemental Hexagrams

There are eight elemental hexagrams, two for each element: invoking and banishing. As mentioned above, however, the four elements have a different meaning in this context than they do in the Ritual of the Pentagram. In that case, the four elements were associated with four stages of creation, and the pentagrams of Earth were associated with the material world. In this case, the four elements are associated with the elemental triplicities in the zodiac. As you can see from this, the Ritual of the Hexagram is inherently stellar, having to do with the extraterrestrial planets and the stars. As such, the stellar elements have a different quality, from those in the pentagram. They are not hierarchical in the same way; there is a correspondence between them. Stellar water shares some qualities with terrestrial water. But they are not the same.

For the simple Ritual of the Hexagram, we use all four elements, in either their invoking or banishing form. The association of the stellar elements with the directions is not based on the four winds (like with the archangels in the Ritual of the Pentagram) but with the cardinal signs of the zodiac. So, in the East we have Fire for Aries ♈; in the South we have Earth for Capricorn ♑; in the West we have Air for Libra ♎, and in the North we have Water for Cancer ♋.

Fire Hexagram

Unlike the other hexagrams, both triangles in the Fire hexagram are pointed upwards, one displaced slightly beneath the other, so that the top of the lower triangle is in the middle of the upper triangle. Begin with the top triangle and go clockwise or anticlockwise depending on if you are invoking or banishing (respectively).

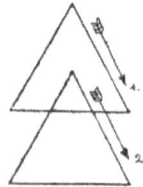

Earth Hexagram

As in many cases in the Golden Dawn system, there is overlap between the element of Earth and the planet Saturn. It is, perhaps, ironic that the furthest planet from us is the one most associated with *terra firma*, but there are a few reasons why this is so. For one, Saturn rules the dead, and the bodies of the dead are beneath our feet. For another, the energy of Saturn is the densest of all the planets, and therefore relates to the solidity of Earth. For yet another, there is a Qabalistic link between Binah and Malkhut. They reflect one another in a mysterious way, so it is fitting that the Earth Hexagram is also the Hexagram of Saturn. It is the only one of the four elemental hexagrams that looks like a normal hexagram. You begin at the top, going clockwise or anti-clockwise depending on whether you are invoking or banishing, as always.

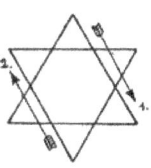

Air Hexagram

The Air hexagram has an upwards and downwards triangle, like the Earth Hexagram, but in this case, they are placed such that their bases overlap, forming a diamond. As before, begin at the top and go clockwise or anti-clockwise depending on whether you are invoking or banishing.

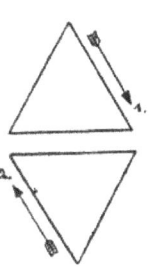

Water Hexagram

The Water hexagram has the two points of the triangles coinciding, so it looks like an hourglass. Begin with the upper (downward pointing) triangle. As always, clockwise is invoking, anti-clockwise is banishing.

ARARITA

In addition to INRI, IAO, and LVX, there is one more *notarikon*, or acronym in this ritual. It is the Hebrew ARARITA which stands for "Echad Rash, Echudotoh Rash, Yechuotoh Rash, Tehmurahtoh Echad", which means "One is God's beginning, one principle is God's individuality, God's permutation is one." It is a seven-lettered name, standing for seven words. Seven, being the number of classical planets, makes this word particularly suited to the Ritual of the Hexagram. It is a reminder that while we encounter the divine in diverse manifestations (as planets, sephirot, and so on) the source of that divinity is one.

Performance

Formulating the hexagrams follows much the same pattern as the formulation of the pentagrams, only in that case, we used the same pentagram in each direction and changed the name. In this case, we use a different hexagram in each direction, but the same word: ARARITA.

As always, begin in the East. Draw the hexagram of Fire. Perform the sign of the enterer, vibrating the word "ARARITA", projecting it through the hexagram. Then perform the sign of silence, to seal it. Carry the light around to the South and do the same thing with the Earth hexagram. Likewise with Air in the West and Water in the North.

Finally, you may repeat the Analysis of the Keyword (above) or the Qabalistic Cross. Here is the entire ceremony in summary:

1. Analysis of the Keyword
    a. "I.N.R.I."
    b. "**Yod, Nun, Resh, Yod**" *(trace* ינרי *from right to left)*
    c. *(extend your arms in the form of a +)* "The sign of Osiris slain."
    d. *(making sign of L)* "The sign of the mourning of Isis."
    e. *(making sign of V)* "The sign of Typhon, Apophis."
    f. *(making sign of X)* "The sign of Osiris risen."
    g. *(repeat sign of L)* "L"

    h. *(repeat sign of V)* "V"
    i. *(repeat sign of X)* "X"
    j. *(vibrate loudly)* "**LUX**"
    k. *(making sign of +)* "the light…"
    l. *(making sign of X)* "…of the cross"
    m. "Virgo, Isis, Mighty Mother"
    n. "Scorpio, Apophis, Destroyer"
    o. "Sol, Osiris, Slain and Risen"
    p. *(raising voice and intensity)* "Isis, Apophis, Osiris"
    q. *(slowly, raising arms)* "**IAO**"
    r. *(slowly lower arms)* "Let the divine light descend."
2. Formulate the Hexagrams
    a. Advance to the East and trace the Hexagram of Fire—with the sign of the enterer, vibrate "**ARARITA**".
    b. Advance to the South and trace the Hexagram of Earth—"**ARARITA**".
    c. Advance to the West, trace Hexagram of Air—"**ARARITA**".
    d. Advance to North, trace Hexagram of Water—"**ARARITA**".
3. Analysis of the Keyword (again) or Qabalistic Cross.

Divination

What is divination, and how is it different from fortune telling? Diviners and fortune tellers both use the same tools (especially Tarot), but in very different ways. Fortune tellers claim to be able to tell you the future.

Then they use techniques like "cold reading", which basically amounts to making statistically informed guesses and measuring your reaction. Since most people who go to a fortune teller want to believe that their fortunes can be told, they will tend to focus on the things the fortune teller gets "right" and conveniently forget what they get wrong. To quote Dr. Leonard Orr: "Whatever the Thinker thinks, the Prover will prove." For fortune tellers, Tarot cards are merely props and have no value in and of themselves. They use them only because they carry an aura of mystique around them that people have come to associate with such powers as these.

Divination is quite different. The purpose of divination is to get in touch with the divine. We can think of divinities as aspects of the self or the unconscious that transcend the ego. They are the faces of vast psychic powers that we can scarcely comprehend. They often know things you (that is, your ego) do not (consciously, anyway). This is where divination comes in.

Divination is a set of techniques whereby we can access that wisdom through the language of symbols. The oldest and most organic form of divination is dream interpretation. All other forms of divination are essentially methods by which to construct what are essentially waking dreams for the purpose of interpretation. They also provide the ability to generate a sort of shared dream with another person to help them access their own divine wisdom.

Astrology

Whether you believe in Astrology or not, it is valuable to understand its symbols. Along with Qabalah, it is one of the key sources for correspondences within this system. The Tarot can be understood as a synthesis of Astrology and Qabalah. Geomancy, likewise, can be understood as a translation of Astrological principles onto the Earth. A deep dive into Astrology is beyond the scope of this text, but there are two principal components worth knowing. First are the seven classical planets. These were discussed in the chapter on the Ritual of the Hexagram. The others are the 12 signs of the Zodiac.

Zodiac

The Zodiac derives from 12 constellations of stars that range across the ecliptic. From the Earth's point of view, the ecliptic describes the path of the Sun across the sky. From the Sun's point of view, it is the plane on which the Earth rotates around the Sun. Each constellation corresponds with a sign. When a planet (including the Sun or the Moon) passes through the segment of the ecliptic associated with that sign, it is considered to be "in" that sign. So, if you were born in "the sign of Aries", that means that the Sun was in Aries at the time that you were born.

> SIDEREAL VERSUS TROPICAL ASTROLOGY
>
> When the associations of the signs of the Zodiac were determined, thousands of years ago, it was observed that the Sun would enter the sign of Aries around the time of the Vernal Equinox. That is, at that time, if you were able to see the stars behind the Sun on the first day of Spring, you would see the constellation of Aries.
>
> Over the thousands of years that have elapsed since that time, as our solar system has rotated through the galaxy, the constellations of the zodiac have also rotated. Over the millennia, the constellation behind the Sun at the time of the Vernal Equinox has shifted. This is called the precession of the Equinoxes.

As a result, there are now two ways of determining the placement of the signs of the Zodiac. One is called the Sidereal method. This has to do with the placement of the actual constellations. This is the system used in Vedic Astrology, popular in India. So in this system, if you were born a day after the Vernal Equinox, you would be a Pisces, not an Aries.

The system more commonly used in the West is the Tropical method. It associates the signs of the Zodiac with the parts of the solar year. So Aries always begins at the Vernal Equinox. Libra always begins at the Autumnal Equinox. In this system, the link between the signs of the zodiac and their constellations is merely historical.

As a matter of fact, it is not as though each constellation were exactly 30 degrees across anyway. Some constellations are bigger than others. Some stretch across the ecliptic while others are more perpendicular to it. Indeed, there is even a 13th constellation, nestled in there, between Scorpio and Sagittarius, called Ophiuchus. In the Sidereal method, this 13th constellation is typically ignored, and the 12 signs are evened out, so even then, a planet may be "in" one sign, but if you were to actually look at the stars behind that planet, you might see the edge of a different constellation.

Some astrologers and magicians do work with the constellations as they actually are. But in our tradition, we work with the Tropical zodiac.

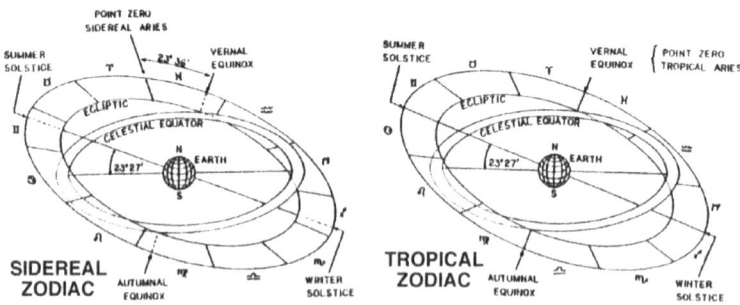

Sidereal vs Tropical Zodiac

[https://www.whitelotusoflight.com/blog/sidereal-vs-tropical-zodiac-and-why-it-matters]

The 12 signs are divided into 4 triplicities, one for each element. You'll recall, in the Ritual of the Hexagram, we discussed these four celestial elements and how they differ from the terrestrial elements utilized in the Ritual of the Pentagram. The Fire signs are Aries, Leo, and Sagittarius. The Earth signs are Taurus, Virgo, and Capricorn. The Air signs are Gemini, Libra, and Aquarius. The Water signs are Cancer, Scorpio, and Pisces.

The triplicities are cardinal, fixed, and mutable. The signs rotate through each modality and each element respectively:

	Cardinal ♀	**Fixed ☉**	**Mutable ☿**
Fire △	Aries ♈	Leo ♌	Sagittarius ♐
Earth ▽	Capricorn ♑	Taurus ♉	Virgo ♍
Air △	Libra ♎	Aquarius ♒	Gemini ♊
Water ▽	Cancer ♋	Scorpio ♏	Pisces ♓

The signs used in the Ritual of the Hexagram are the cardinal signs (as in the cardinal directions).

Sun and Moon

Most people these days, even if they don't know anything about Astrology, know their Sun sign. This is partially because it's so easy to reckon as it can be easily determined by your birthday, though it can get confused if you are born on the cusp and the equinox comes a little early or a little late that year. But for the most part, it's pretty straight forward.

The sign of the Moon can be reckoned fairly easily without an ephemeris if you know the phase of the Moon. If it's a new Moon, that means the Moon is in the same sign as the Sun. If it's a full Moon, that means it's opposite the Sun. So, if it's a full Moon, and the Sun is in Aries, that means the Moon is in Libra, and vice versa. If it's a waxing Half Moon, and the Sun is in Aries, then the Moon would be in Cancer, that is, 1/4 of the way around the Zodiac from Aries.

Other planets are harder to reckon without some sort of help. However, Mercury and Venus, being inner planets, are never too far from the Sun. Mercury in particular is almost always within one sign of the Sun. So, if the Sun is in Aries, Mercury will almost certainly be in Pisces, Aries, or Taurus.

> **WHAT IS MERCURY RETROGRADE?**
>
> These days people talk a lot about Mercury Retrograde. All the planets (including Mercury) only go in one direction around the Sun. But from the point of view of the Earth, it can sometimes *seem* as though Mercury was moving backwards. This can happen with other planets too, but most often comes up with Mercury. Since Mercury is the God of communication, many believe that when Mercury is retrograde communication is more likely to be confused.

Ascendant and Houses

Aside from the position of the planets in the signs, there are a few more aspects of Astrology that come up. One is the Ascendant. This is simply the sign that is on the horizon at the time in question. If you were born at sunrise, then your Ascendant would be the same as your Sun sign. If you were born at sunset, then it would be the opposite sign. If you were born at moonrise, then your Ascendant would be the same as your moon sign, and so on. Your Ascendant is not a planet, but in Astrological charts, it is almost as though it were treated as such.

The Ascendant marks the start of the first house of twelve. Somewhat counterintuitively, the houses progress downwards. This is because they follow the progression of the signs of the zodiac. So if your first house is Aries (that is, you were born with Aries on the horizon in the East) then your second house would be Taurus, and so on. The 7th house would be above the horizon to the West and the 12th house would be above the horizon to the East.

Houses (and Ascendant) do not come up much in Magick, except that some magicians will time their workings to correspond with when a planet is in a particular house. Any book on Astrology will go into more detail on houses, so I will leave it at that.

Tarot

The Tarot consists of 78 cards divided into Major and Minor Arcana. The Major Arcana are 22 Trumps that are associated with powerful archetypes. The 56 Minor Arcana cards are divided into four suits of 14 cards each. Each suit contains 10 "pip" cards, numbered Ace through 10 and 4 Court Cards. If the Minor Arcana sound a lot like traditional playing cards, that's no mistake. The Tarot is an elaboration on traditional playing cards, only instead of three court cards per suit (King, Queen, and Jack), there are four (King, Queen, Knight or Prince, and Princess); and instead of just one trump card (the Joker) there are 22. The origin of Tarot is unknown. Ancient origin stories to the contrary, it appears they were invented in the late 14th century as a game, and only later began to be used for divination.

Major Arcana

It was Eliphas Levi who first popularized the notion that the 22 trumps, or Major Arcana, were tied to the 22 letters of the Hebrew alphabet (or aleph-bet). In his system, the first letter Aleph (א) corresponds with trump I, the Juggler or Magician; Bet (ב) with II, the Popess or High Priestess, Gimel (ג) with III and so on. The 0 card, the Fool, was associated with the letter Shin (ש) in his system.

The Golden Dawn iterated on this, but changed the correspondences, so 0 (the Fool) became Aleph, I (the Magician) became Bet, II (the High Priestess) became Gimel, and so on. This can get a bit confusing because Aleph (א) also corresponds with the number 1, so 0=1, I=2, II=3, and so on until IX=10 (Yod) and X=20 (Kaph) but it is, at least, consistent.

Crowley changed the associations again, according to instructions he received in the Book of the Law, switching the associations for Heh and Tzaddi.

To my knowledge, no one today uses Levi's associations. (Of course, it's a big world, and so *someone* must. But I have not come across it outside of Levi's own writings.) The other two systems though, the Golden Dawn's and Crowley's, are both in wide usage. The Golden Dawn's correspondences are the ones used in A.E. Waite's deck (formerly known as the Rider-Waite deck, giving credit to Waite and his publisher, Rider; now more properly known as the Smith-Waite deck, to give credit to Waite and the actual illustrator of the deck, Pamela Coleman Smith). Though Waite did not explicitly indicate the Golden Dawn associations, they deeply influenced his and Smith's designs, both of whom were members of the original Golden Dawn. The Smith-Waite deck has become the prototype for virtually every Tarot deck since.

Crowley published his version in the Book of Thoth. His deck was also based on the Golden Dawn correspondences, with a few alterations, the biggest change being the one mentioned above, swapping the correspondences of Heh and Tzaddi. He also renamed many of the trumps, though this was hardly new. Already, by the time the cards reached the Golden Dawn, the Juggler had become the Magician, the Pope had become the Hierophant, the Popess had become the High Priestess, and so on. Crowley changed other cards in accordance with his own theology, changing the Last Judgment to Aeon and Strength into Lust, for example. Most modern decks are based either on Smith-Waite's or on Crowley's, or sometimes a blend of the two.

Correspondences

According to *Sepher Yetzirah*, the letters of the Hebrew aleph-bet are divided into three categories: mothers, doubles, and simples. There are three mother letters: Aleph (א), Mem (מ), and Shin (ש). They correspond with the primordial elements Air, Water, and Fire respectively. You might be surprised to see the element of Earth missing from this list.

This is because, in *Sepher Yetzirah*, the letters are said to generate the Universe, and the Earth is not generative, but receptive. That said, Earth does correspond with the letter Tav (ת) which, though a double letter, does have some mother letter characteristics.

The seven double letters are so-called because they each have two pronunciations. (Students of modern Hebrew may be confused by this since not all of the double letters have two pronunciations today and some of the other letters do. But for our purposes, we will ignore that fact and stick with what is described in Sepher Yetzirah.) The seven double letters are Bet (ב), Gimel (ג), Dalet (ד), Kaf (כ), Pe (פ), Resh (ר), and Tav (ת). These correspond with the seven planets, though not in a traditional order. If you read Aryeh Kaplan's translation of Sepher Yetzirah, you will see that there have been many competing correspondences according to different rabbis over the centuries. For our purposes, we will stick with the Golden Dawn correspondences listed below.

The twelve simple letters remain, and they correspond to the twelve signs of the zodiac. For the most part, these correspondences are in the order you would expect, with Heh (ה) corresponding with Aries, Vav (ו) with Taurus, Zayin (ז) with Gemini and so on.

However, when developing the *Book of Thoth*, Aleister Crowley made some adjustments. In particular, he switched the association between the Emperor/Aries (IV) and the Star/Aquarius (XVII) so in his version, the Emperor corresponds with Tzaddi, while the Star corresponds with Heh. He also swapped the order of VIII and XI but not the correspondences. So, Strength (or, in his version, Lust) still corresponds with Tet and Leo, it's just now card XI instead of VIII; while Justice (or Adjustment) is still Lamed/Libra, but is now VIII instead of XI.

Atu		Letter	Meaning	Association	Tarot Card	
O	א	Aleph	Ox	Air	Fool	△
I	ב	Bet	House	Mercury	Magician	☿
II	ג	Gimel	Camel	Moon	Priestess	☽
III	ד	Dalet	Door	Venus	Empress	♀
IV (or XVII)	ה	He	Window	Aries (or Aquarius)	Emperor (or Star)	♈
V	ו	Vav	Nail	Taurus	Hierophant	♉
VI	ז	Zayin	Sword	Gemini	Lovers	♊
VII	ח	Chet	Fence	Cancer	Chariot	♋
VIII (or XI)	ט	Tet	Serpent	Leo	Strength (or Lust)	♌
IX	י	Yod	Hand	Virgo	Hermit	♍
X	כ	Kaf	Palm	Jupiter	Fortune	♃
XI (or VIII)	ל	Lamed	Ox Goad	Libra	Justice (or Adjustment)	♎
XII	מ	Mem	Water	Water	Hanged Man	▽
XIII	נ	Nun	Fish	Scorpio	Death	♏
XIV	ס	Samek	Prop	Sagittarius	Temperance (or Art)	♐
XV	ע	Ayin	Eye	Capricorn	Devil	♑
XVI	פ	Pe	Mouth	Mars	Tower	♂
XVII (or IV)	צ	Tzadi	Fish-hook	Aquarius (or Aries)	Star (or Emperor)	♒
XVIII	ק	Qof	Back of Head	Pices	Moon	♓
XIX	ר	Resh	Head	Sun	Sun	☉
XX	ש	Shin	Tooth	Fire	Judgment (or Æon)	△
XXI	ת	Tav	Tau	Saturn	Universe	♄

Correspondences according to Book T, with Crowley's adjustments given in parentheses.

These 22 letters (and their respective cards) can then be placed on the Qabalistic Tree of life we introduced earlier. As with the correspondences of the 7 doubles, there are a variety of ways one might place these letters on the 22 paths between the 10 sephirot. Again, we will focus on the associations used by the Golden Dawn while calling out changes made by Aleister Crowley. The order is, in a way, fairly straightforward, in that it begins at the top with Aleph (the Fool) being the bridge between the first two sephirot: Keter and Chokmah, and continues downward such that the last letter, Tav (the Universe) forms the bridge between the last two sephirot: Yesod and Malkhut.

One thing worth calling out though is how Crowley's changes affect this, particularly on the path between Netzach and Yesod, which is Tzaddi. Traditionally, this would correspond with the Star (Aquarius) but in *the Book of Thoth*, this becomes the Emperor (Aries). Interestingly, he did not modify the placement of Strength/Lust and Justice/Adjustment. So those still correspond with the paths between Chesed and Gevurah and between Gevurah and Tipharet as before. It is just the card numbers which are swapped.

Pathworking

We'll discuss this more in a later chapter, but it's worth mentioning at this point that the sequential placement of the cards on the Qabalistic Tree contributes to something called the Path of Return. The idea here is that the Tree is analogous to Jacob's Ladder, stretching from Earth (Malkhut) to Godhead (Keter). We can approach God by ascending this tree. We can do this by working with the cards in reverse order, starting with Tav, then Shin, then Resh, then winding over to Qoph, and so on. This is also called the Path of the Serpent because of how it winds its way back and forth as it climbs the Tree.

Supernal Triad

We won't go into every card in detail, but there are several worth highlighting. First is what might be thought of as the supernal triad of cards. Just as there is a supernal triad of sephirot, consisting of the first three sephirot, the first three cards have a similar primordial quality. They correspond with the paths between Keter and Chokmah, Binah, and Tipharet respectively.

The Fool is the first, or rather, the zero-th card. It is the only card from the Major Arcana that also exists in regular playing cards as the Joker. It corresponds with the Hebrew letter Aleph, one of the three Mother letters alluded to above. Unlike the other two (Mem) and (Shin), Aleph has no sound of its own. (It is typically transliterated as 'A' in the Roman alphabet, but that's not really accurate. It only has the "a" sound when paired with the "a" vowel point (ָ), for example, אָ.) This is a fitting representation of the ineffable, unspeakable, that exists between Wisdom (Chokmah) and Will (Keter). It is beyond, before, or between all categories.

The Magician corresponds with the letter Bet (ב). The Torah begins with the letter Bet in the word Bereshit, which translates to "in the <u>b</u>eginning..." It connects the Crown (Keter) with

Understanding (Binah) which, unlike Wisdom (Chokmah) is capable of being put into words. It is also the primordial seed, expressive of will descending into manifestation. It is the Wand.

The High Priestess corresponds with the letter Gimmel (ג). She lies on the path from the Crown (Keter) down to Tipharet (Beauty). Tipharet is the heart of the Tree of Life. It sits at the nexus, connecting nearly all of the other sephirot excepting Malkhut, which is separated from Tipherat by Yesod. Both Yesod and the High Priestess correspond with the Moon which tells us that the Moon can be a key to higher wisdom. It has been said that the waters that flow from her dress are the source of all rivers that occur throughout the Tarot, such as in the Temperance card discussed below.

THE HIGH PRIESTESS

Inner Gateway

Tipharet is the heart of the Tree of Life, sitting as it does halfway between Godhead in the Crown (Keter) and us in the Kingdom (Malkhut) on Earth. It corresponds with your Holy Guardian Angel. Some say that achieving Knowledge and Conversation with your Holy Guardian Angel is or should be the primary goal of Magick, because it is through that that you can come to know and achieve your own true Will. However, before you can reach that, you must overcome three ordeals represented

TEMPERANCE.

by three cards: Death, the Devil, and the Tower, corresponding with Nun (נ), Ayin (ע), and Peh (פ) respectively. If you look on the Tree of Life you will see that these three letters form a triangle beneath Tipharet. Between them is threaded Samek (ס) corresponding with Temperance. Death represents fear, particularly fear of death. An Adept must overcome their fear of death. The Devil represents enslavement to appearances. Finally, the Tower represents the illusion of separateness. The path of Samekh (Temperance or Art) between them represents balance and the alchemical transformation that occurs through this process.

Outer Gateway

One last card I want to mention is the World or Universe card, corresponding with the final letter, Tav (ת). Tav represents both Saturn and the Earth, referencing a hidden connection between Malkhut and Binah. It represents completion. It is also the first obstacle that must be overcome when ascending Jacob's Ladder in the form of the Tree of Life.

Integrating the Major Arcana

You may find it valuable to first work with the cards in the forward order, beginning with the Fool and ending with the Universe. One of the best ways to do this is to start with line drawings of the cards which you can then color in. The Builders of the Adytum sells a pack of their version of the Smith-Waite deck specifically for this purpose. You can also simply use an existing deck (preferably one based upon either the Smith-Waite deck or the Thoth deck). Otherwise, you can always make your own following the guidelines in the Appendix. In fact, creating your own deck is the best, but also the most difficult. Spend at least a day working with each card in turn. Spend some time just looking at it, seeing what you notice, trying to notice every detail. While I can't say this for every Tarot deck, for the Smith-Waite deck and for the Thoth (or Crowley-Harris) deck, every detail is symbolic. Nothing is accidental.

So, try to take it all in. For the day or week that you are working with a card, keep it in the back of your mind. Keep an eye out for how its energy manifests in the world around you.

Minor Arcana

The Minor Arcana tends to get short shrift in most discussions of the Tarot, and I'm afraid that, in true Golden Dawn fashion, I will not depart from that tradition. Of course, most of the cards (56 out of 78) are Minor Arcana cards. The meaning of the Minor Arcana cards, as with the Major Arcana, is derived from both Qabalistic and Astrological correspondences. However, unlike the Major Arcana, in which these correspondences are relatively pure, in the Minor Arcana, they become mixed. Each suit corresponds with one of the four elements: Pentacles with Earth, Swords with Air, Cups with Water, Wands with Fire. (I've heard that some flip the association of Swords and Wands. But in the Golden Dawn, these are the correspondences.) The pips—that is, the numbered cards—correspond with the ten sephirot. So, the Ten of Pentacles is Malkhut of Earth. The Six of Cups is Tipharet of Water.

The Astrological correspondences are more complicated. Each of the pips, 2 through 10, correspond with both a planet and a sign. The signs are simple enough. Wands correspond with Fire signs, Cups correspond with Water signs, *etc.* 2, 3, and 4 correspond with the cardinal signs, 5, 6, and 7 with fixed signs, and 8, 9, and 10 with mutable signs. So the 2 of Wands corresponds with Aries. The 6 of Cups corresponds with Scorpio.

The planetary correspondences are where it gets complicated. It follows the same order we've discussed in the Middle Pillar and Ritual of the Hexagram, that is, the Chaldean order, from the outside in. That is: Saturn, Jupiter, Mars, the Sun, Venus, Mercury, the Moon. (So far, we've mostly used the reverse order, from inside-out.) So if the 5 of Wands is Saturn, then the 6 of Wands is Jupiter, the 7 of Wands is Mars, and all of these being in the sign of Leo. We then move on to Earth with the 8 of Pentacles corresponding with the Sun (in Virgo), 9 with Venus, and 10 with Mercury. Then we move on to Air, starting over with 2, so the 2 of Swords corresponds with the Moon (in Libra). The 3 of Swords then goes back to Saturn (again, in Libra). The 4 with Jupiter, and so on.

To be honest, I've always found the correspondences of the planets with the pips difficult to remember. Crowley was considerate enough to include the symbols for these attributions on the cards themselves. (I suppose not even he could remember all of them.) If you are particularly conversant in Astrology, then these correspondences can be of use. But for the rest of us, we are more likely to find value in the names the Golden Dawn (and Crowley) attached to each of these cards interpreting these correspondences, or, better yet, the images Smith designed for them. After all, which is more evocative, Mercury in Capricorn? Or an image of three women cheerfully raising their cups together?

Playing Cards

What if you don't have access to a Tarot deck? Fortunately, most of the cards in the Tarot can be found in a simple deck of playing cards. Of course, this excludes all but one of the Major Arcana (the Fool is the Joker). Another difference is that the Tarot has four court cards for each suit while a typical playing card deck has just 3: King, Queen, and Jack. This changes the associations somewhat, but with a little creativity, we can generate correspondences based on our understanding of Tarot and Astrology. For example, one thing you could do is associate Kings with the fixed signs (Leo, Scorpio, Aquarius, and Taurus), Queens with mutable signs (Sagittarius, Pisces, Gemini, and Virgo), and Jacks with cardinal signs (Aries, Cancer, Libra, and Capricorn). We'll also need to find a correspondence between the playing card suits and those in Tarot. I've seen multiple correspondences, but the one that that works for me is: Clubs for Wands (in many of the Smith-Waite cards, the wands in fact look more like clubs), Hearts for Cups (both relate to emotion), Spades for Swords (both are pointy), and Diamonds for Pentacles (which are often rendered as Coins, both representing material forms of wealth). So, in this system, the King of Clubs would be Fixed Fire, or Leo. The Queen of Hearts would be Mutable Water, or Pisces. The Jack of Spades would be Cardinal Air, or Libra. This is, of course, just one of many ways you could use Tarot correspondences with regular playing cards; there are other entirely distinct ways of using playing cards for divination. One popular approach is Lenormand, named after Marie Anne Lenormand who famously used playing cards for divination. The traditional Petit Lenormand uses only 36 cards. The meaning of these cards has no connection to Tarot or Qabalah as far as I can tell.

Divination Spreads

There are numerous ways of laying out cards, often called spreads, for divination purposes. There are two that I use frequently. The first is a simple three card spread which can be used to give a kind of "weather report" for the situation in question. There are any number of associations you could apply to the three cards, but perhaps the most straight-forward is past-present-future.

The one thing I don't like about this spread, and in fact, most spreads I've come across, is that they don't do anything to account for choice on the part of the querent (the person you're reading for). It can seem fatalistic, suggesting "this is your future no matter what". Of course, that's never the case. The very fact that you are utilizing divination can change the outcome of a situation. But spreads like this do nothing to account for that reality.

I have, however, come across one spread that does, and I like it very much. It's specifically designed for weighing two options. It's important, before beginning, to identify which is the first, or default option, and which is the second, or alternative option. It's a 15-card spread, far more complicated than the three-card spread described above. However, in principle, it's actually fairly simple (far simpler than the famous 10-card Celtic Cross spread, for instance). In it, you lay out a kind of X consisting of five groups of three cards as shown on the following page.

Each section has one card representing it with two cards modifying it. (This is also a way to do the three-card spread, with simply one card as the focus of the reading with two cards on either side modifying it.) Modification cards emphasize and interact with the primary card. If the modification cards are contrary to the primary card, that indicates a kind of blockage, like how many readers interpret reversals. (Note, when using this method, I do not use reversals, as the modification cards serve the same purpose. If a card comes up reversed, I just flip it right-side-up.)

12) external modifier	10) default or first option	11) internal modifier				15) external modifier	13) alternative or second	14) internal modifier
			3) outer influence	1) current situation / state of mind	2) inner influence			
9) external modifier	7) external (social) influence	8) internal modifier				6) external modifier	4) un-conscious influence	5) internal modifier

The three cards in the center represent the querent's current situation or state of mind. The three cards in the lower right represent internal—usually unconscious—influences. The three in the lower left represent external—generally social—influences. The three cards in the upper left represent the outcome in the first or default case. The three cards in the upper right represent the outcome in the second or alternative case. Often, it's clear, just from looking at these, which choice would have the desired outcome. The other cards effectively tell you why.

This spread works just as well with playing cards as with Tarot cards.

Geomancy

The third and final form of divination I will discuss here is Geomancy. Compared to Astrology and Tarot, Geomancy is comparatively easy and requires few tools. One need only learn to recognize sixteen symbols (compared to the 78 cards in the Tarot or the 64 hexagrams in the *I Ching*). It is also extremely versatile, requiring nothing more than a pencil and paper.

While Geomancy is practically unknown in the modern world, in the Middle Ages, it was perhaps the most popular form of divination. In those days, casting an Astrological horoscope was extremely difficult, requiring an ephemeris. These days, anyone with a computer can cast a chart, though interpreting the horoscope can still be a challenge. When Tarot cards became easy to acquire, that became a popular method for divination, particularly with decks like the Waite-Smith deck providing imagery to assist in the interpretation so nearly anyone can simply pick up a deck and use their intuition to produce a decent reading. But Geomancy remains a largely (in my opinion) underrated form of divination which can often give more clear and precise answers than either Astrology or Tarot.

Constructing a Shield Chart

The first step is to divine the four mothers. Since each figure is a combination of four rows, this means coming up with sixteen (that is, 4 rows x 4 mothers) random numbers. In the olden days, this would be done by making sixteen rows of dots in the sand. The idea would be to go into a bit of a trance, so you lose track of how many dots you are putting down. Then, at the end, you count how many dots are in each row. If it's even, that's 2. If it's odd, that's 1.

. . . .	= 36 dots → 2	. .
. . . .	= 33 dots → 1	.
. . . .	= 41 dots → 1	.
. . . .	= 38 dots → 2	. .

Later this was adapted to making dots on paper with a pencil or pen. But then people realized that you could get similar results by taking a handful of beans, and counting whether you picked up an even or an odd number. You could also use dice. Ana Cortez describes a method of using playing cards. She counts Jacks as 11, Queens as 12, and Kings as 13. The problem with this is that playing cards (unlike Tarot cards) have an odd number in each suit, making it more likely to get an odd number than an even number. One could solve this problem by simply removing the Court cards from the deck. You could also, of course, use coins. One method I've started to use employs a stopwatch, timing the length of a breath and looking at the number of milliseconds. The point is, there are an infinite number of ways to get 16 random numbers. But if all you have is pencil and paper, the dots-on-paper method is traditional and will do in a pinch.

You construct the figures from the top down, and arrange them from right to left. The first four numbers become the first Mother, the next four, the second Mother, and so on. These four then become the four Daughters by, essentially, rotating them 90 degrees. The top row of the first Mother becomes the top row of the first Daughter. The top row on the second Mother becomes the second row on the first Daughter. The top row on the third Mother becomes the third row on the first Daughter. The top row on the last Mother becomes the bottom row on the first Daughter. The second row on the first Mother becomes the first row on the second Daughter, and so on.

Mothers				
..	.	..	..	1
..	.	..	.	2
.	.	..	.	3
.	..	..	..	4

	4	3	2	1
Daughters	..	.	.	..
	..	..	..	..
	..	.	.	.
	.	.	..	..

You now have eight figures: four Mothers and four Daughters. You now combine them in pairs to become the four Nieces. The first two Mothers combine to become the first Niece. Rows are calculated just as before: totaling the dots: if it's even–two, if it's odd–one. So, the top row of the first two Mothers both have 2 dots, totaling to 4. 4 is even, so that becomes 2 on the first row of the first Niece. The second row has 1 and 2, totaling 3. 3 is odd, so the second row of the first Niece is 1, and so on. The last two mothers become the second Niece. The first two Daughters (consisting of the top two rows of the four Mothers) combine to become the third Niece, and so on.

These four Nieces are again combined, in pairs, to become the right and left Witness, respectively. Finally, the two Witnesses are (you guessed it) combined to form the Judge.

The Daughters, Nieces, and Witnesses are laid out as follows, starting with the first Mother in the top right corner:

	Daughters	Mothers
Nieces		
Witness		
	Judge	

Due to the way the figures are combined, there are only 8 possible Judges. So, when learning the figures, I recommend you start with those. They are known as "impartial" figures. The Judge gives the final outcome of the reading. If we want more nuance, we look at how it was constructed.

First, we go back and look at the two Witnesses. Each Witness can be constructed from one of sixteen combinations of figures. The one on the left represents the outer world. The one on the right represents the inner world. The two Witnesses can further be analyzed by considering how they were constructed from the four Nieces.

An alternative to the shield chart is the house chart, which uses the same method to derive the figures, but arranges them into the twelve houses of Astrology. There are different methods of doing this, from the most straightforward—where the first Mother is the first house, the second is the second, the Daughters are assigned to houses 5 through 8, and the nieces to 9 through 12—as well as more elaborate methods, placing the Mothers in the 1st, 4th, 7th, and 9th house, for instance. I won't elaborate on this further as I find the shield method more than adequate. But it's worth knowing that other methods exist should you come across them.

As mentioned above, there are 16 possible figures that can be generated from four binary options. However, an interesting effect occurs when the figures are combined and recombined to form the Judge such that there are only 8 possible Judges. Those are called impartial, and the remaining eight are partial.

The Impartial Figures

The Impartial Figures all have an even number of dots. They are possible Judges.

Via & Populus

Via and Populus are the two simplest figures, each consisting of the same line repeated four times. They are 100% active (in the case of Via) or 100% passive (in the case of Populus).

Via

Via is the simplest of the four figures, consisting of four single dots, and it symbolizes a Road, representing movement and change. It is also arguably the most transformative figure, as it changes any figure it interacts with into its opposite. For example, Amissio (Loss) becomes Acquisitio (Gain) ... and vice versa. Likewise, it is formed by the union of opposites. It is good when change is good, and bad when change is bad.

Populus

Populus is the next simplest. It is the opposite of Via, consisting of four pairs of dots. It means "People". Whereas Via transforms any figure it interacts with into its opposite (including itself), Populus keeps it the same. Likewise, it is formed by the combination of two of the same figure. I think of Populus as a kind of amplifier. Like Via, it is good when the situation is good, and bad when the situation is bad.

Amissio & Acquisitio

Amissio and Acquisitio have alternating active and passive elements. They represent Loss and Gain respectively.

Amissio

Amissio represents Loss. The figure represents a bag turned over, emptying out. It is good when you're trying to lose something, but bad otherwise.

Acquisitio

Acquisitio represents Gain. The figure represents a bag getting filled from the top. It is good in most situations, particularly when there is something you want to come to you, but bad when you are trying to get rid of something.

Fortuna Major & Minor

Fortuna Major and Minor both represent good fortune of varying degrees.

Fortuna Major

Fortuna Major means Great Fortune. It is the image of a valley through which a river flows. It is good in all situations and represents the best-case scenario.

Fortuna Minor

Fortuna Minor means Lesser Fortune, but that can be misleading. What it really means is something that appears good on the surface, but there is some caveat, something that is wrong. The image is a mountain with a staff atop it. This may indicate a good outcome, but be careful.

Conjunctio & Carcer

Conjunctio and Carcer are the last of the impartial figures and represent more nuanced outcomes.

Conjunctio

Conjunctio means Conjunction. It represents a bringing together. The figure represents a crossroads or two joining figures. It is good when the question is about the joining of people (as in a marriage or partnership) or recovering of things. Otherwise, it may indicate that this is needed in order to achieve a good outcome.

Carcer

Carcer means Prison. The figure is an enclosure or a link in a chain. It indicates immobility and potentially isolation. It is generally bad, but can be good in situations where isolation or a lack of movement is called for. For example, if you are being moved around a lot against your will, Carcer could indicate an end to that movement, which could come as some relief.

The Partial Figures

The Partial Figures each have an odd number of dots. Due to the combination of Mothers and Daughters, Nieces and Witnesses, it is impossible for a partial figure to be a Judge. However, one or both (or neither) of the Witnesses can be partial. Thus, understanding the partial figures can help provide nuance to the reading if needed. Furthermore, all 16 figures can be used Magickally to change the outcome of a situation. For example, if you want to transform Carcer into Via, you could invoke the power of Conjunctio. More on that below.

Laetitia & Tristitia

Laetitia and Tristitia are emotional symbols, indicating sorrow and joy, so by their nature they are partial.

Laetitia

Laetitia means Joy. It is the image of an arch, fountain, rainbow, or tower. If it is the Left Witness, it may indicate something that brings others joy that plays a role in the final outcome. If it is the Right Witness, it may indicate something that brings the querent joy. Though positive in itself, the outcome is determined by how it combines with the other witness.

Tristitia

Tristitia means Sadness. It is the image of a pit, a broken arch, or a stake being driven into the ground. If it is the Left Witness, it may indicate something that brings others sadness that plays a role in the final outcome. If it is the Right Witness, it may indicate something that brings the querent sadness. Though generally negative, the outcome is determined by how it combines with the other witness.

Puer & Puella

Puer and Puella represent the masculine and feminine energies at their extreme examples.

Puer

Puer means Boy. The figure represents a sword or erect phallus. It represents unmediated masculinity. It may indicate aggression, passion, and even war. As the Left Witness, it may represent a man, or more generally, aggression in another person or in systems of power. As the Right Witness, it may represent the querent's own boyish qualities.

Puella

Puella means Girl. The figure represents a vulva, a woman with exaggerated breasts, or a mirror. It represents femininity. It may represent peace and passivity. It could also represent friendliness. Like Puer, it has an immature quality and may represent fickleness. As the Left Witness, it may represent a woman, or alternatively, a friendly or passive quality in the situation. As the Right Witness, it may represent the querent's own girlish qualities.

Caput & Cauda Draconis

The binary of Caput Draconis and Cauda Draconis is a pair representing the beginning and the end.

Caput Draconis

Caput Draconis means "Head of the Dragon". The image is of a doorway with steps leading to it. It represents beginnings. It indicates something that has just started or is about to start.

Cauda Draconis

Cauda Draconis means "Tail of the Dragon." The image is of a doorway with steps leading away from it. It represents endings. It indicates endings. In some traditions, if this figure was revealed as the first mother, the reading would be stopped immediately. As a Witness, it represents something that has ended or is about to end.

Albus & Rubeus

Albus and Rubeus are another emotional pairing—Serenity and Passion. Again, it is important not to label them as "good and "bad"; both have their place.

Albus

Albus means "White". It represents peace and detachment. The image is of an upright glass or goblet. In some ways, it is like a more mature or developed Puella. It is generally positive in itself, but depending on its placement in the chart, could be unhelpful, particularly when action is needed.

Rubeus

Rubeus means "Red". The image is of an overturned glass or goblet. It represents passion and could represent a more extreme form of Puer. Whereas Puer could be an out-of-control boy, Rubeus could be a full-grown man who still has not learned to control his temper. In some traditions, like Cauda Draconis, if it were revealed as the first Mother, the reading may be stopped immediately.

Associations

Each of the Geomantic figures has elemental, planetary, and zodiac associations. I intentionally omitted them from the initial discussion of them as I have found it more valuable to learn to relate to the figures on their own before complicating them with these other associations. Until you've learned to relate to Albus as Albus, the associations are more likely to distract and confuse you. Each of the figures has a spirit. I recommend you either spend some time meditating on the spirit of each figure or doing some readings, or both, in order to get a sense of how the figures work and interact with each other prior to studying their elemental, planetary, and zodiacal associations.

Here they are, presented in alphabetical order:

	Inner Element	Outer Element	Planet	Sign
Acquisitio	Air △	Fire △	Jupiter ♃	Sagittarius ♐
Albus	Water ▽	Air △	Mercury ☿	Gemini ♊
Amissio	Fire △	Earth ▽	Venus ♀	Taurus ♉
Caput Draconis	Earth ▽	Earth ▽	North Node ☊	Virgo ♍
Carcer	Earth ▽	Earth ▽	Saturn ♄	Capricorn ♑
Cauda Draconis	Fire △	Fire △	South Node ☋	Sagittarius ♐
Conjunctio	Air △	Earth ▽	Mercury ☿	Virgo ♍
Fortuna Major	Earth ▽	Fire △	Sun ☉	Leo ♌
Fortuna Minor	Fire △	Fire △	Sun ☉	Leo ♌
Laetitia	Fire △	Water ▽	Jupiter ♃	Pisces ♓
Populus	Water ▽	Water ▽	Moon ☾	Cancer ♋
Puella	Water ▽	Air △	Venus ♀	Libra ♎
Puer	Air △	Fire △	Mars ♂	Aries ♈
Rubeus	Air △	Water ▽	Mars ♂	Scorpio ♏
Tristitia	Earth ▽	Air △	Saturn ♄	Aquarius ♒
Via	Water ▽	Water ▽	Moon ☾	Cancer ♋

As discussed, each figure consists of four rows. The rows correspond to the elements from top to bottom: Fire, Air, Water, Earth. The elements are either active or passive, depending on whether there are one or two dots respectively. You'll notice that the inner element of each figure is always one of the active elements of the figure (except for Populus which has no active elements).

Another thing you might notice is the "planet" for the Caput Draconis and Cauda Draconis are not planets *per se* but rather the North

Node and South Node respectively. The North Node and South Node are the two points where the orbit of the Moon intersects the ecliptic (the ecliptic is the apparent path of the Sun). The North Node is also known as the ascending node or sometimes *caput draconis*. The South Node is the descending node or *cauda draconis*. Though they are not actual astronomical bodies but rather points calculated by the intersection of two circles, they are often used in astrological readings as though they were planets.

Geomantic Magick

As mentioned above, one thing you can do with Geomantic figures is invoke them to transform a situation. I gave the example of transforming Carcer into Via, by invoking the power of Conjunctio. First, it will help to have a good sense of all three figures and the spirits behind them to help you feel how Conjuntio transforms Carcer into Via (and how it can also work the other way). Then I might work on invoking both the outer element corresponding with the sign of the figure, along with its planet. So in the case of Conjuntio, that would be Earth (Virgo) and Mercury. First prepare an altar with the symbol for Conjunctio. You could draw it on a piece of paper or lay out six stones in the figure's shape. If you draw it, you may like to embellish it. People often connect the dots to form a kind of sigil. Clear the space using the LBRP. Then invoke the celestial influences using the Invoking Ritual of the Hexagram. Then invoke Mercury, specifically, with the Hexagram of that planet (see the chapter on Practical Magick below on details for how to do this). Finally draw that energy down with an Invoking Ritual of the Pentagram of Earth. Then meditate on the symbol and feel the presence of the spirit of Conjunctio in the space. Ask it to transform Carcer into Via.

(Note: I have never actually tried this ritual. If I had, it is likely I might try it a few times and make adjustments according to what feels right. What works for you may not work for another. You may wish to simplify or embellish it. I simply offer this as an example of the kind of work you can do with these symbols.)

Example Reading

The querent asked whether they should join a particular group.

| puer | puer | conjunctio | fortuna minor |

| populus | amissio |

| amissio |

Interpretation

Judge: Amissio – Loss – Interpretation: joining this group would lead to loss. Don't do it.

Right Witness: Amissio – Loss – This is due partially to a loss the querent is already experiencing.

Left Witness: Populus – People – The people in this group would only amplify the loss already experienced.

Third and Fourth Nieces: Both Puer – Boys – This is because of the immaturity and ego of the people involved in the group.

Summary: In short, the querent would be advised not to join the group as it will lead to disappointment and loss owing to a prior loss the querent had already experienced combined with a general immaturity in the group in question which would only make things worse.

Analysis: In fact, the querent was considering joining this new group because of frustration and disappointment in a previous group they were already a member of. Considering this, it becomes less clear whether the left witness and the third and fourth nieces refer to the new group in question or the old group or both. Either way, joining this new group would not be a good idea at this time. In fact, once the new group discovered the relationship with the previous group, they rejected the querent.

Interlude:
A History of
Ceremonial Magick

Historical Roots

As you are now introduced to the three core rituals of this curriculum, you might find it useful to know where all of this came from. As discussed in the introduction, the elements of Ceremonial Magick come from the Medieval European grimoire tradition—including elements of both Qabalah and Hermetism—along with a strong dose of Rosicrucianism and Alchemy. Each of these elements is worthy of study in their own right, but a brief overview will help orient you to the tradition.

The Grimoire Tradition

First, the Medieval European grimoire tradition. A grimoire is essentially a recipe book for spells. For the most part they were handwritten (and hand-copied) manuscripts detailing all kinds of methods for producing certain results, from cures and curses as well as a variety of other goals. Many of these can trace their origin to the pre-Christian Mediterranean region. One of the most important collections of these are known collectively as the *Papyri Graecae Magicae*, abbreviated PGM, or Greek Magical Papyri. The PGM contains numerous eclectic spells utilizing a mixture of Pagan and Abrahamic (that is, Jewish—or, later, Judeo-Christian) God-names. One of these rituals is known as the Headless One, which became the Bornless One, an important ritual for Adepts in the Golden Dawn tradition (see Appendix).

Magick has always been on the edge, from the pre-Christian Mediterranean to medieval Europe. Sometimes Magick was tolerated, sometimes it was seriously persecuted. Often it was done by people who lived on the fringes, but sometimes it was picked up by people in power. Many of the manuscripts from the medieval era were composed by Christian monks and priests. Two of the most important medieval grimoires include the Key of Solomon and the Lesser Key of Solomon.

These were translated into English by Samuel Liddell "MacGregor" Mathers, one of the founding members of the Order of the Golden Dawn. They, too, were used extensively by the Adepts of his Order.

Qabalah

Qabalah, also spelled Kabbalah and Cabala, is a mystical tradition born out of a series of books written (most likely) in the thirteenth century known collectively as the *Zohar*. The *Zohar* was written by Jews in Spain and provides a mystical interpretation of the first five books of the Bible (the Torah). Mystical Judaism goes back much farther than that, and elements of it can be seen in the PGM mentioned above, as well as (importantly) a small book known as *Sepher Yetzirah*, which was probably written around the 3rd or 4th century, and was translated into English by William Wynn Westcott, another one of the founding members of the Golden Dawn. However, it wasn't until the *Zohar* that Qabalah as we know it really came into being.

Qabalah was picked up by Christians and Hermeticists in the late medieval period. It has become a convention to use different spellings depending on which tradition we are talking about. If we're talking about the Jewish tradition, we will typically spell it "Kabbalah". If we're talking about the Christian tradition, we'll spell it "Cabala". Finally, if we are talking about the Hermetic tradition, we'll spell it "Qabalah". Since this book concerns itself primarily with the Hermetic tradition, we'll be spelling it "Qabalah" throughout. If I ever use the spelling, "Kabbalah," it will indicate that I am referring to it in its Jewish context. It is highly unlikely that you will ever see me spell it "Cabala".

Hermetism and Hermeticism

In the classical era, there was a movement we call Hermetism. This produced such works as the *Corpus Hermeticum*, which had a major impact on later Renaissance philosophers and spawned what we now call Hermeticism. Hermeticism differs from Hermetism in that it syncretizes developments from Qabalah, Alchemy, and Rosicrucianism. Hermeticism is the core philosophy of the Order of the Golden Dawn, so much so that it is often referred to as the Hermetic Order of the Golden Dawn.

Alchemy

A full treatment of alchemy is beyond the scope of this book, but the core concept of alchemy is also essential to it. Alchemy is ultimately about transmutation. It is commonly thought of as a (perhaps foolhardy) attempt to turn base metals (especially lead) into gold. Symbolically, we can understand this as turning the base materials of the self into something divine. When the Golden Dawn talks about becoming "more than human" (see Part II), this is what they are talking about.

Rosicrucianism

Rosicrucianism began as a series of manifestos that were released in Germany in the 17th century, which referred to a Brotherhood of the Rosy Cross. Whether this fraternity actually existed, or if the whole thing was just a giant hoax, is still debated. What is definitely true, however, is that whether or not such a Brotherhood existed prior to these documents being written, they most certainly did afterwards. People reading these documents wanted it to exist and went out searching, and when they didn't find what they were looking for, they created it. Over time, Rosicrucian orders came into existence. I am not aware of any Rosicrucian order that can trace its lineage prior to the publication of the so-called Rosicrucian manifestos. Be that as it may, these would-be Rosicrucian fraternities have had a tremendous influence on the Western Mystery Tradition ever since. The Inner Order of the

Golden Dawn is profoundly Rosicrucian in nature. There are also numerous other Rosicrucian orders. Perhaps the most famous is the Ancient Mystical Order Rosae Crucis or AMORC.

The Hermetic Order of the Golden Dawn

The Order of the Golden Dawn sat at the nexus of all of these movements. It was the inheritor of ancient knowledge stretching from the Greek Magical Papyri to the Rosicrucian manifestos, from the *Corpus Hermeticum* to the *Zohar*. It synthesized these into a reasonably coherent system of initiation and Magick. This then, through the work of Israel Regardie, Aleister Crowley, and many others, became the template for later developments of what is collectively known as the Western Mystery Tradition. The very idea, in modern paganism, of casting a circle and calling in the elements, owes itself to the Golden Dawn. That isn't to say that the Golden Dawn was the only tradition that ever did this. Native American and Tibetan traditions are both known for doing similar things, though with different elemental attributions. But if you put Air in the East, Fire in the South, Water in the West, and Earth in the North (as most modern witches do), there's a pretty good chance that your tradition got that from the Golden Dawn. It's valuable to know the history of the Golden Dawn both to understand the context within which this magickal system was developed, and also as a warning to would-be Magickal orders.

The Order of the Golden Dawn was formed in 1888 by three British Freemasons who were all members of the Societas Rosicruciana in Anglia (S.R.I.A.): William Wynn Westcott, Samuel Liddell "MacGregor" Mathers, and William Robert Woodman. The S.R.I.A. is what's known as an appendant body of Freemasonry, meaning that you must be a 3° Freemason to join it. Since Freemasonry in England (and in the rest of the English-speaking world) admits men only, this means the S.R.I.A. is effectively men-only.

The story goes that William Wynn Westcott received a manuscript written in code from his friend, the Rev. A. F. A. Woodford, who received it from Kenneth Mackenzie (also a member of S.R.I.A.) who supposedly found it in a book in a library. The actual origin of the manuscript is unknown. What is known is that Westcott decoded the manuscript which provided an outline for a series of initiatory rituals as well as some notes about Tarot and Qabalah. (It may be noted, as an aside, that encoding Masonic rituals in a cipher is very common. One can easily find books of Masonic rituals written in cipher for sale on the Internet.)

The decoded rituals and notes became the basis of what we today call the Hermetic Order of the Golden Dawn. The initiatory structure of the Order was similar to that of the S.R.I.A. There were, however, several important differences—the first being that initiates were taught certain practices, while the S.R.I.A. remains theoretical. Perhaps as important, they removed certain requirements from membership, chiefly being a Mason (and therefore a man) and being a trinitarian Christian (also a requirement of the S.R.I.A.) While the Golden Dawn remained ultimately Rosicrucian, it did not require its members to be of the Christian faith. Also, by dropping the requirement of being a Mason, it was able to admit women.

The Order survived just over a decade, however, before splintering and falling apart. The first major hit was the loss of William Robert Woodman, who died in 1891 due to a sudden illness, just as the Golden Dawn was getting its start. It is unknown how much he might have contributed to the Order, but with his death, one of the three legs that formed the foundation of the Order was kicked out, leaving Westcott and Mathers.

The next big loss came in 1896 when a Golden Dawn manuscript was found in a cab that Westcott had taken, thus revealing his membership in the secret society and involvement in the occult. This was seen as unseemly, given his role as Crown Coroner, and so he was forced to resign from the Order so that he might keep his job.

This left only Mathers, with no one else to temper him. By then, he had already moved to Paris (in 1892) and was left trying to keep the growing Order under control from across the English Channel. While Mathers was arguably a genius in occult matters, his organizational skills would seem to have left something to be desired, because within a few years of Westcott's death, the Adepts of the English and Scottish temples revolted against Mathers. The Order ultimately fell apart around the turn of the 19th century. But out of the ashes were born a number of new Orders, perhaps most notably the Stella Matutina, which is the one Israel Regardie was a member of and thus the source of most of our information about the Magickal practices of the Golden Dawn.

The Order of the Golden Dawn in the Outer

It's interesting to note that in the original Order manuscripts, it did not call itself the Hermetic Order of the Golden Dawn, but rather, the Order of the Golden Dawn in the Outer. It has been said that the Golden Dawn did not actually teach Magick. Whether this is true or not depends on your definition of Magick, but it is true that it did not teach practical Magick. Those lessons were reserved for the Inner Order, which I will describe below. The Outer Order was meant to be preparatory. The Cipher Manuscripts outlined 5 grades, which corresponded with the same four grades in the first order of the S.R.I.A., with one preparatory grade attached—that is: Neophyte, Zelator, Theoricus, Practicus, and Philosophus. The four grades from Zelator through Philosophus correspond with the four lowest sephirot on the Qabalistic Tree (Malkhut, Yesod, Hod, and Netzach). Since these are the 10th, 9th, 8th, and 7th sephirot respectively, that is what leads to the peculiar designation of the grades: Zelator is 1=10 (*i.e.* the 1st grade corresponding with the 10th sephirah), Theoricus is 2=9, and so forth.

Neophyte, arguably the most important of these grades, is 0=0. That is, it is the zero-th grade (if you will) and does not correspond with any sephirah. I say it is the most important because it is not only the initiation into the entire system, but it also forms the template for the practical Magick undertaken by Adepts in the order.

To this system of five grades was added one more: Portal. Portal, like Neophyte, does not correspond to any sephirah. It is, rather, a bridge between the Order of the Golden Dawn in the Outer, and the Inner Order, known as the R.R. et A.C. The R.R. et A.C. had grades corresponding with the three second order grades of the S.R.I.A., namely Adeptus Minor, Adeptus Major, and Adeptus Exemptus. Like the Outer Order grades, they also correspond with the sephirot, so they are indicated as 5=6 (*i.e.* 5th grade, 6th sephirah or Tipharet), 6=5, and 7=4.

The Order of R.R. et A.C.

The Ordo Rosae Rubeae et Aureae Crucis, or Order of the Rose of Ruby and Cross of Gold, was the so-called Inner Order of the Golden Dawn. While the grades of the Outer Order were modeled after the Cipher Manuscripts, the Inner Order degrees were developed later. The first of these degrees, 5=6, or Adeptus Minor, is included among the rituals presented in most exposés of the Golden Dawn rituals, including Israel Regardie's. While the Portal ritual is essentially a recap of the four elemental grades (1=10 through 4=7), the Adeptus Minor ceremony is quite different. Both are thought to have been originally composed by Mathers.

One thing that immediately becomes apparent in the R.R. et A.C. is how distinctly Rosicrucian it is. While the Outer Order is predominantly Hermetic, in this ceremony, the aspirant goes through a ceremony modeled after the Rosicrucian manifestos. That is to say, it is deeply Christian, albeit in a way that most Christians probably wouldn't recognize. It is worth noting however that one need not be a Christian in the regular sense to receive Rosicrucian teachings. The Christ, in this context, is meant to represent an archetypal quality available to all humans, regardless of what you believe about the historical Jesus.

Manuscripts refer to the Adeptus Minor grade being subdivided into the same four elemental grades in the Outer Order: Zelator, Theoricus, Practicus, and Philosophus. A fair bit can be found on the study materials for Zelator Adeptus Minor (frequently abbreviated Z.A.M.) Less can be found on Theoricus Adeptus Minor (Th.A.M.) I have yet to see anything written on the latter two. My understanding is that there were no ceremonies to mark the transition through the subgrades of Adeptus Minor. You merely graduated to the next level when you were deemed ready.

Later, initiation ceremonies were devised for the higher grades, Adeptus Major (6=5) and Adeptus Exemptus (7=4). However, given how few people make it this far, there is not much written on the subject. The best book that I have found is called *Beyond the Sun* by Nick Farrell.

Subsequent Orders

Orders die, but their members move on, and often found orders of their own. From the original Golden Dawn were born at least two new Orders: Alpha et Omega and Stella Matutina. Stella Matutina is particularly important because that is the Order that Israel Regardie joined. It was, in fact, the Stella Matutina (not the Golden Dawn) documents that Regardie published under the title *The Golden Dawn*. By the time the materials had come to Regardie, much had been added to the original.

The Stella Matutina was also the source of the Smaragdum Thallasses Temple in New Zealand which operated all the way up until 1978. It is thanks to this temple that we have much of the more advanced material such as the higher grades, alluded to above, as well as deeper analyses of the Outer Order rituals published by Pat Zalewski.

As for Alpha et Omega, it is through them that we get Dion Fortune—who founded the Fraternity of the Inner Light—and Paul Foster Case—who founded the Builders of the Adytum. Both of these Orders are still in existence (though the Fraternity of the Inner Light has since renamed itself the Society of Inner Light). Both of these Orders offer correspondence courses. The Builders of the Adytum are particularly focused on the Tarot, so if that is of interest to you, it may be worth checking out.

Of course, no discussion of the offspring of the Golden Dawn would be complete without mentioning the Beast himself, "Uncle Al"—Aleister Crowley. I once heard the advice that it is better to read Crowley's own writings before reading anything about him; the reason being that if you know too much about the man, it is likely to taint your appreciation of his writings. It's worth mentioning that Aleister Crowley's involvement with the Golden Dawn did nothing to help its longevity and may have contributed to its downfall. Crowley became the protege of Mathers in France, but the English members of the Golden Dawn would not have him. Yeats, when commenting on why he believed Crowley was not a suitable member of the Golden Dawn, remarked that the Order was "not a reformatory." Crowley, for his part, believed that Yeats was merely jealous of Crowley's superior poetry. (History has clearly judged otherwise.)

As a result, Crowley did not have regular experience of the Golden Dawn, though he was technically a member. He received most of his instruction directly from Mathers. Then in 1904 he had a strange experience in which he received what is now known as *the Book of the Law* of *Liber AL vel Legis* from an entity calling itself Aiwass, whom he identified as his Holy Guardian Angel. This was the foundation of the religion known as Thelema, which is far more popular today than it ever was during Crowley's lifetime. He went on to found a new order—the A∴A∴ (not to be confused with Alcoholics Anonymous—quite the contrary!) The history of this Order beyond Crowley's death is murky at best, with multiple groups claiming lineage from the original.

Part 2:
More than Human

It has been said that the goal of the Golden Dawn system of Magick is to make the aspirant "more than human." This is, arguably, the "Great Work" or Magnum Opus of the Alchemists and Philosophers. What does this mean? The way I understand it, it means transcending the limitations of the "I" or "ego". Please don't misunderstand me. I am not one of those people who believes the "ego" is bad, but it is limited. The part of your brain that constructs your sense of identity, that is your sense of "I", is really very small. Your consciousness accounts for just an infinitesimal fraction of what you are capable of. To become "more than human" means to open your experience to that which is greater than yourself. This is the goal of an Adept.

Inner Work

To reach this goal, we must go within. The work of the Magician takes place predominantly in the imagination. From a Qabalistic standpoint, the imagination could be attributed to the sephirah of Yesod, one step above Malkhut, below all that occurs above it. It is like the interface between the potential and the actual. When you attempt to work Magick in the world, you form your desire in the imaginal and then bring it into the material. However, at this point, we are still operating primarily between these two lowest points. For this reason, this form of Magick is often called "Low Magick". To go beyond Yesod, we must engage with our imagination in a different way. Rather than forming our desires in our imagination, in which case the imagination is the passive receptacle of our intention, we instead go the other way. We allow those powers that exist beyond our consciousness to speak to us through the imagination, and in this way, the imagination becomes active. This is why Carl Jung called this process "Active Imagination".

Active Imagination

Engaging with the imagination in this way is tricky. It is easy to get into a state where you're wondering, "Am I making all of this up?" And once you've gone beyond that, "Is this all just random?" At first it will probably feel as though you are making all of it up, but with practice, you will begin to be surprised by what you experience. This should be an indication that it is not "you", or at least, not your egoic desires, making it up anymore—but just because it surprises you doesn't necessarily mean it's meaningful. It must be coherent, not random. Here you will need to exercise some discernment. Because it can be difficult to be both receptive and discerning at the same time, one practice is to simply allow it all to happen, write it down, and then afterwards judge whether it was nonsense or not. Another technique is to test your vision. I will come back to that shortly.

There are two techniques I learned for developing active imagination from a Jungian analyst, and they can each be done in two ways. The two techniques are: 1) engaging in dialogue and 2) imagining what happens next. The two are related. In fact, you might think of engaging in dialogue as really a special case of "what happens next," but it's important enough to treat on its own. The two ways are with fairy tales, and with dreams.

Dialoguing is a deceptively simple but effective technique. Here is an example, taken from *the Red Book* by Carl Jung in which he imagined himself in a desert, following a path to an anchorite (represented "A" below, while Jung is "I"):

I: *"Am I disturbing you, father?"*

A: *"You do not disturb me. But do not call me father. I am a man like you. What is your desire?"*

I: *"I come without desire. I have come to this place in the desert by chance, and found tracks in the sand up there that led me in a circle to you."*

A: *"You found the tracks of my daily walks at daybreak and sunset."*

I: "Excuse me if I interrupt your devotion; it is a rare opportunity for me to be with you. I have never before seen an anchorite."

A: "There are several others whom you can see further down in this valley. Some have huts like me, others live in the graves that the ancients have hallowed out in these rocks. I live in the uppermost in the valley, because it is most solitary and quiet here, and because here I am closest to the peace of the desert."

There are a couple things I'd like to point out about the above snippet. First, Jung engages with his unconscious as though it were totally real. He does not treat the anchorite as if he were his own creation, but rather as an independent entity. By doing so, the anchorite can tell him things he didn't already know. Second, the anchorite is able to explain aspects of his vision that Jung did not previously understand (the tracks in the desert). Third, the anchorite can tell him about what he might experience should he venture further.

In my own active imagination experiments, the dialogues are usually the most valuable part. But this sort of dialogue is not limited to what you can do when you venture into the inner world. It can also be done in normal waking consciousness, even with inanimate objects or places. In fact, speaking with the land can be an incredibly fruitful activity that can help you better connect with the land on which you live.

Fairy Tales

Fairy tales may seem an unlikely tool in Magick. They are just for children, right? But in fact, these folk tales, many of which have been around for centuries, perhaps longer, have deep roots in our collective unconscious. It could be said that Disney's whole empire is founded upon the fact that they figured out a way to commodify these ancient and primordial tales, distorting them just enough to give them intellectual property rights, but retaining that connection to those deep archetypes within us. In modern Western storytelling (including all Disney movies) the story is usually tied up rather neatly at the end with no loose ends. But in older tales, this is less often the case. There are often tons of loose ends, and this makes for good material to engage the imagination. So, when you have some quiet time, read this story ... and at the end, think about what happens next. Give it some time and let the characters do what seems natural. Don't try to force it in any direction. Let it unfold naturally. Then, if you like, engage in a dialogue with one of the characters. Ask her why she did something, and see what answer comes to mind. Don't worry if it just feels like you're making it up. Let it flow and see what happens. Below is an example of a fairy tale chosen for this purpose:

> **THE NIXIE IN THE POND BY JACOB AND WILHELM GRIMM**
>
> [retrieved from https://sites.pitt.edu/-dash/grimm181.html on August 24, 2023]
>
> Once upon a time there was a miller. He lived contentedly with his wife. They had money and land, and their prosperity increased from year to year. But misfortune comes overnight. Just as their wealth had increased, so did it decrease from year to year, until finally the miller scarcely owned even the mill where he lived. He was in great distress, and when he lay down after a day's work, he found no rest, but tossed and turned in his bed, filled with worries.
>
> One morning he got up before daybreak and went outside, thinking that the fresh air would lighten his heart. As he was walking across the mill dam, the first sunbeam was just appearing, and he heard something rippling in the pond.
>
> Turning around, he saw a beautiful woman rising slowly out of the water. Her long hair, which she was holding above her shoulders with her soft hands, flowed down on both sides, and covered her white body. He saw very well that she was the nixie of the pond, and he was so frightened that he did not know whether to run away or stay where he was. But the nixie, speaking with a soft voice, called him by name and asked him why he was so sad.

At first the miller was speechless, but when he heard her speak so kindly, he took heart and told her how he had lived with good fortune and wealth, but that now he was so poor that he did not know what to do.

"Be at ease," answered the nixie. "I will make you richer and happier than you have ever been before. You must only promise to give me that which has just been born in your house."

"What else can that be," thought the miller, "but a young dog or a young cat," and he promised her what she demanded.

The nixie descended into the water again, and consoled and in good spirits he hurried back to his mill. He had not yet arrived there when the maid came out of the front door and called out to him that he should rejoice, for his wife had given birth to a little boy.

The miller stood there as though he had been struck by lightning. He saw very well that the cunning nixie had known this and had cheated him. With his head lowered he went to his wife's bed. When she said, "Why are you not happy with the beautiful boy?" he told her what had happened to him, and what kind of a promise he had given to the nixie.

"What good to me are good fortune and prosperity," he added, "if I am to lose my child? But what can I do?"

Even the relatives who had come to congratulate them did not have any advice for him.

In the meantime, good fortune returned to the miller's house. He succeeded in everything that he undertook. It was as though the trunks and strongboxes filled themselves of their own accord, and as though money in a chest multiplied overnight. Before long his wealth was greater than it had ever been before. However, it did not bring him happiness without concern, for his agreement with the nixie tormented his heart. Whenever he passed the pond he feared she might appear and demand payment of his debt.

He never allowed the boy himself to go near the water. "Beware!" he said to him. "If you touch the water a hand will appear, take hold of you, and pull you under."

However, year after year passed, and the nixie made no further appearance, so the miller began to feel at ease.

The boy grew up to be a young man and was apprenticed to a huntsman. When he had learned this trade and had become a skilled huntsman, the lord of the village took him into his service. In the village there lived a beautiful and faithful maiden whom the huntsman liked, and when his master noticed this, he gave him a little house. The two were married, lived peacefully and happily, and loved each other sincerely.

One day the huntsman was pursuing a deer. When the animal ran out of the woods and into an open field, he followed it and finally brought it down with a single shot.

He did not notice that he was in the vicinity of the dangerous millpond, and after he had dressed out the deer, he went to the water in order to wash his blood-stained hands. However, he had scarcely dipped them into the water when the nixie emerged. Laughing, she wrapped her wet arms around him, then pulled him under so quickly that waves splashed over him.

When it was evening and the huntsman did not return home, his wife became frightened. She went out to look for him. He had often told her that he had to be on his guard against the nixie's snares, and that he did not dare to go near the millpond, so she already suspected what had happened. She hurried to the water, and when she found his hunting bag lying on the bank, she could no longer have any doubt of the misfortune. Crying and wringing her hands, she called her beloved by name, but to no avail. She hurried across to the other side of the millpond, and called him anew. She cursed the nixie with harsh words, but no answer followed. The surface of the water remained calm; only the moon's half face stared steadily back up at her.

The poor woman did not leave the pond. With fast strides, never stopping to rest, she walked around it again and again, sometimes in silence, sometimes crying out loudly, sometimes sobbing softly. Finally her strength gave out, and she sank down to the ground, falling into a heavy sleep. She was soon immersed in a dream.

She was fearfully climbing upwards between large rocky cliffs. Thorns and briers were hacking at her feet. Rain was beating into her face. The wind was billowing her long hair about. When she reached the top a totally different sight presented itself to her. The sky was blue, a soft breeze was blowing, the ground sloped gently downwards, and in a green meadow, dotted with colorful flowers, stood a neat cottage. She walked up to it and opened the door. There sat an old woman with white hair, who beckoned to her kindly.

At that moment, the poor woman awoke. It was already daylight, and she decided at once to follow her dream. With difficulty she climbed the mountain, and everything was just as she had seen it during the night. The old woman received her kindly, showing her a chair where she was to sit.

"You must have met with misfortune," she said, "having sought out my lonely cottage."

The woman related with tears what had happened to her.

"Be comforted," said the old woman. "I will help you. Here is a golden comb for you. Wait until the full moon has risen, then go to the millpond, sit down on the bank and comb your long black hair with this comb. When you are finished, set it down on the bank, and you will see what will happen."

The woman returned home, but the time passed slowly for her until the full moon came. Finally the shining disk appeared in the heavens, and she went out to the millpond, sat down, and combed her long black hair with the golden comb. When she was finished she set it down at the water's edge. Before long there came a motion from beneath the water. A wave arose, rolled onto the bank, and carried the comb away with it. In not more time than it took for the comb to sink to the bottom, the surface of the water parted, and the huntsman's head emerged. He said nothing, only looking at his wife with sorrowful glances. That same instant a second wave rushed up and covered her husband's head. Then everything vanished. The millpond lay as peaceful as before, with only the face of the full moon shining on it.

Filled with sorrow, the woman returned, but she saw the old woman's cottage in a dream.

The next morning she again set out and told her sorrows to the wise woman. The old woman gave her a golden flute, and said, "Wait until the full moon comes again, then take this flute.

Sit on the bank and play a beautiful tune on it. When you are finished, set it in the sand. Then you will see what will happen."

The woman did what the old woman had told her to do. No sooner was the flute lying in the sand than there was a motion from beneath the water, and a wave rushed up and carried the flute away with it. Immediately afterwards the water parted, and not only her husband's head, but half of his body emerged as well. He stretched out his arms longingly towards her, but a second wave rushed up, covered him, and pulled him down again.

"Oh, what does it help me," said the unhappy woman, "for me only to see my beloved and then to lose him again?"

Despair filled her heart anew, but a dream led her a third time to the old woman's house. She went there, and the wise woman gave her a golden spinning wheel, comforted her, and said, "Everything is not yet fulfilled. Wait until the full moon comes, then take the spinning wheel, sit on the bank, and spin the spool full. When you have done this, place the spinning wheel at the water's edge, and you will see what will happen."

The woman did everything exactly as she had been told. As soon as the full moon appeared she carried the golden spinning wheel to the bank, and spun diligently until she was out of flax, and the spool was completely filled with thread. She had scarcely placed the wheel on the bank when there was a more violent motion than before from the water's depth. Then a powerful wave rushed up and carried the wheel away with it.

Immediately the head and the whole body of her husband emerged in a waterspout. He quickly jumped to the bank, caught his wife by the hand, and fled. They had gone only a little distance when the entire millpond arose with a terrible roar, then with terrible force streamed out across the countryside. The fugitives saw death before their eyes, when the wife in her terror called out for the old woman to help them, and they were instantly transformed, she into a toad, he into a frog.

The flood which had overtaken them could not destroy them, but it separated them and carried them far away. When the water receded and they both reached dry land again, their human forms returned again, but neither knew where the other one was. They found themselves among strange people who did not know their native land. High mountains and deep valleys lay between them. In order to earn a living, they both had to herd sheep. For long years they drove their flocks through fields and woods, and were filled with sorrow and longing.

One day when spring had once again broken forth on the earth, they both went out with their flocks, and as chance would have it, they moved toward one another. He saw a herd on a distant mountainside and drove his sheep toward it. They met in a valley but did not recognize one another, but they were happy that they were no longer so alone. From then on every day they drove their flocks next to each other. They did not speak much, but they did feel comforted.

One evening when the full moon was shining in the sky, and the sheep were already at rest, the shepherd took his flute out of his pocket and played on it a beautiful but sorrowful tune. When he had finished he saw that the shepherdess was crying bitterly.

"Why are you crying? he asked.

"Oh," she answered, " the full moon was shining like this when I played that tune on the flute for the last time, and my beloved's head emerged out of the water."

He looked at her, and it was as though a veil fell from his eyes. He recognized his beloved wife, and when she looked at him, with the moon shining on his face, she recognized him as well. They embraced and kissed one another, and no one needed to ask if they were happy.

Dreams

You can do the same thing with your own dreams. The first step, of course, is to remember your dreams. Some of us do this already naturally, but others have difficulty. The easiest way to remember a dream is to wake up in the middle of it. It's always unpleasant to be woken up in the middle of a dream, but if you can make it happen (say, with an alarm) it is an almost sure-fire way to be able to remember your dream. If you are woken up spontaneously, try to remember not to go back to sleep right away, but to remember your dream. If possible, write it down. This will tell your brain that remembering your dreams is important (even more important than going back to sleep!) so with practice, you will start remembering your dreams without having to be woken up in the middle of them. If possible, always keep a pencil and notebook by your bed so you can record your dreams the moment you wake up. Do this even if you think you don't remember anything. Write down the date and try to remember something, anything. Even if it's just an image or a feeling and write it down. If you really can't remember anything at all, just write that you don't remember anything. Eventually your unconscious will get the picture that this is important to you and will start to help you remember your dreams.

Once you've got a dream, do the same thing you did with the fairy tale above. Ask yourself, "What happens next?" and see what comes up. Or imagine one of the characters in the dream before you, and ask them a question. If you are writing this in your dream journal, indicate where the dream ends and the imagination begins, as you may want to refer back to this later and it may be useful to know which was which. This technique can be particularly valuable if you have an encounter in a dream and want to see where it might have gone if you kept dreaming. Perhaps they had something to tell you. Now is their chance.

Testing the Vision

This brings up the question of whether your experience is just wish fulfillment or is actually valuable. Again, you can save that question until after you have recorded the dream or vision. At that point, you should go back over it and really ask yourself, is this just something you wanted to hear? Is it obvious? Is it coherent? This will help you identify when you may actually be in conversation with something higher than yourself.

The other thing you can do (and this is more valuable when doing Pathworking—which we explain below—but can also be done in dreams if you are lucid) is to test an entity in a vision. This is particularly important when you meet someone who claims to be a certain entity, like the archangel Michael, for instance. You can test them by giving them the Sign of the Enterer (see the chapter on the Ritual of the Pentagram). The other being should respond to that with the Sign of Silence. If they don't, if they balk or try to get out of it, you know you are dealing with an imposter. Cast the sign of the Pentagram between you and them and banish them.

Now, it may seem odd that this works. What if you meet someone claiming to be Athena? Why would Athena respond with the Sign of Silence? Remember, this is all occurring through the medium of your imagination. Just as Athena is not really a person—she just appears to you as such in your vision—she is not *really* giving the Sign of Silence. Rather, she is interacting with you in a way that appears as the Sign of Silence. Because this exchange is a Magickal one, imposters cannot imitate it. If that all seems too strange or esoteric, don't worry about it. The point is: it works, even if it doesn't make sense that it should.

Pathworking

The goal of high Magick is to unite the lower self with the higher Self. Qabalistically, this means ascending the Tree of Life as if it were Jacob's ladder leading from Earth to Heaven. We've discussed the ten sephirot of the Tree of Life in the chapter on the Middle Pillar. Between these 10 sephirot are 22 paths corresponding with the 22 letters of the Hebrew alphabet (or aleph-bet) and simultaneously with the 22 cards of the Major Arcana in the Tarot. There are different arrangements of the paths on the Tree of Life but in the Golden Dawn, it follows a simple progression from top to bottom with the first letter, Aleph, forming the path between the first two sephirot (Keter and Chokmah) and the last letter, Tav, forming the path between the last two sephirot (Yesod and Malkhut). The association between the cards of the Major Arcana with the Hebrew letters and paths is similarly simple, with the first (0—the Fool) going with Aleph, and the last (21—the World or the Universe) going with Tav.

> **REARRANGEMENTS OF THE PATHS AND CARDS**
>
> It's worth noting that different traditions use different arrangements of the paths and cards. For instance, a well-known Jewish Qabalist known as the Ari (meaning Lion) placed the letters on the Tree of Life according to the type of letter. More relevant to readers of this book however will be the changes made by Aleister Crowley. Following his reception of the Book of the Law in 1904, he concluded that a couple of the cards needed to be rearranged. The biggest change he made in this respect was switching the associations between the letters—Heh and Tzaddi—and the cards—the Emperor and the Star. Traditionally, Heh, being the 5th letter, would correspond with the Emperor, Atu IV (remember that the cards of the Major Arcana start with 0, so 0 = 1, I = 2, II = 3 and so on). Likewise, Tzaddi is associated with the Star. He came to the conclusion that these two should be reversed: that Heh should be associated with the Star (and with Aquarius) and Tzaddi should be associated with the Emperor (and with Aries). However, on the Tree of Life, he retained the associations with the letters and the paths. So Tzaddi is the path from Netzach to Yesod in either system. In the Golden Dawn, that path is associated with the Star and with Aquarius, but in Thelema, it's associated with the Emperor and with Aries.

As we advance spiritually, following this system, we gradually ascend the Tree of Life, beginning in Malkhut, ascending through the path off Tav to Yesod, and so on. This is called the Path of Return, since we are returning to source, or the Path of the Serpent, since it winds around each branch of the Tree of Life. There are many ways to actualize this ascent, but one of the simplest which can be done alone in your own room is called Pathworking.

There are 32 paths on the Tree consisting of the 10 sephirot and the 22 letters between them. They are ordered such that the first 10 correspond with the sephirot and the latter 22 with the letters. So the 11th path is the first letter, or Aleph, corresponding with the Tarot card, the Fool. This can be a little confusing since that means the 11th path corresponds with the 1st letter and the 0th card. The 21st path corresponds with the 11th letter, Kaf (which has the numeric value 20) and the 10th card, the Wheel of Fortune. The 32nd path corresponds with the 22nd letter, Tau, and the 21st card, the Universe. When pathworking, we gradually ascend, alternating sephirot and letters. So first, you encounter the 10th path of Malkhut, followed by the 32nd path of Tau, followed by the 9th path of Yesod.

These paths are associated with 32 "intelligences" which are described in a document often included with the Sepher Yetzirah which gives us the attributions of the letters with the elements, planets, and signs of the Zodiac. The description of the 32 intelligences that are associated with each of the 32 paths of Wisdom can be helpful to invoke and/or meditate upon before Pathworking. I've included all 32 in an appendix and the relevant passages below.

For the 22 paths associated with Hebrew letters, I have included the associated text for the Tarot card corresponding with that letter from a document known simply as *the Tarot Trumps* attributed to G.H. Soror Q.L. who is thought to be Harriet Miller Davidson. The "G.H." stands for "Greatly Honored", means that she was a member of the Inner Order and probably an officer. The Q.L. likely stands for Quaero Lucem, which means "I seek the Light" in Latin. The original Golden Dawn was truly a secret society and kept the identities of their members secret in order to protect them; recall that one of the founders had to resign once his membership in the Order was discovered. Instead, they would use the initials of a chosen motto. Regardless of G.H. Soror Q.L.'s true identity, her description of the cards may be particularly useful for inspiration during Pathworking. I have reproduced the corresponding texts with the paths below. The complete text can be found in an Appendix.

Pathworking means working the paths of the Tree of Life. In recent years, this term has been expanded to mean any guided meditation where you "go" somewhere. But traditionally, this term specifically refers to this Qabalistic practice. In the Golden Dawn tradition, it typically involves "entering" a Tarot card in your imagination. Before embarking on the

Path of Return, if you haven't already done this you may find it valuable to first work with the cards in the forward order, beginning with the Fool and ending with the Universe. See the chapter on Tarot for instructions. Once you have familiarized with each of the cards in forward order, you are ready to follow the Path of Return beginning in the Temple of Malkhut.

The Temple of Malkhut

We always begin and end our journey in the Temple of Malkhut. The key to the Temple of Malkhut is the name of God associated with this sephira, which we learned as part of the Middle Pillar exercise: *Adonai ha-Aretz*. You can visualize this in any way that makes sense to you utilizing the symbolism of Malkhut. What follows are just some suggestions.

Earth: Malkhut is associated with both the element of Earth and the planet Earth. You may want to visualize the temple in a densely wooded area or in a cave. You might visualize the walls as rough stone or marble or dark wood, for example.

Ten: Malkhut is the 10th sephirah and is therefore strongly associated with the number ten. You might visualize it as a ten-sided temple and/or with a ten-sided altar. Perhaps there are ten pillars or candlesticks.

Black, olive, russet, citrine: These are the colors associated with Malkhut. You may visualize an altar cloth decorated in this way, or banners in the four corners, with black behind you to the West, russet to your left in the North, olive to your right in the South, and citrine ahead of you in the East.

You may encounter the archangel Sandalphon and possibly Metatron, as well as the four archangels you are familiar with from the Ritual of the Pentagram: Michael, Gavriel, Raphael, and Auriel. You may also be introduced to the elementals: salamanders (for fire), undines (for water), sylphs (for air), and gnomes (for earth).

From the 32 Paths of Wisdom:

The Tenth Path is the Resplendent Intelligence, so called because it is exalted above every head, and sits on the throne of Binah [Understanding]. It illuminates the splendor of all the Lights, and causes an influence to emanate from the Prince of Countenances, the Angel of Keter [Metatron].

The Path of Tau - ת

The Path of Tau ת is Saturnine. Initiation into the mysteries always involves facing death, and that is what we must do here.

> In my own first attempts to work this path, I thought it might help to invoke Saturn to unlock this path. In practice, I found this counterproductive. The energy of Saturn weighed me down and made it harder to travel along this path. Instead, I just got a blackness. In retrospect, I would advise you not to do any special invocation to open this path. Perform a simple banishing and simply place an image—either the XXI card of the Tarot if you have one—or a hand drawn letter Tau ת.

Within the Temple of Malkhut, there are three paths ahead of you. The one to the left has the letter Shin: ש. The one to the right has the letter Qoph: ק. The one straight ahead has the letter Tau: ת. You may see the World or Universe card painted on the door or as a curtain.

In many cultures, the land of the dead is across some body of water. For example, in Greece, it's the river Styx. A ferryman carries the souls of the dead across this body of water. It is quite likely you will encounter a similar body of water when you pass through this door. There may be a ferryman to take you across or you may need to pilot the boat yourself. On your way across, you may have visions or encounters in the water or in the sky above.

From the Tarot Trumps:

> *Observe that this represents not the World but the Universe. It should be remembered that to the ancients, Saturn represented the confines of the Solar system. They had no means of measuring either Uranus or Neptune. To them, therefore, Saturn passing through the spiral path of the Zodiac, marked at its cardinal points by the symbols of the Kerubim forming the Cross, was a comprehensive glyph of the whole.*

From the Thirty-two Paths of Wisdom:

> *The Thirty-second Path is the Administrative Intelligence, and it is so called because it directs and associates the motions of the seven planets, directing all of them in their own proper courses.*

The Temple of Yesod

At the end of the Path of Tau is the Temple of Yesod. You know the key to unlocking the Temple of Yesod from your practice of the Middle Pillar. It is *Shaddai el-Chai*. Yesod means foundation, and here you may have a vision of the machinery of the universe. The Temple of Yesod is a lunar place. It also, like the Temple of Malkhut, can have a four-fold quality, only on a higher, or more subtle register. Here you are likely to meet again the archangel Gavriel. In addition to the Moon, it also corresponds with the sky generally and elemental Air as the mediator between Watery Hod and Fiery Netzach.

From the Thirty-two Paths of Wisdom:

> *The Ninth Path is the Pure Intelligence, so called because it purifies the Numerations, it proves and corrects the designing of their representation, and*

disposes their unity with which they are combined without diminution or division.

The Path of Shin - שׁ

Recall the Temple of Malkhut had three doors. Last time we passed through the middle door to the Path of Tau. This time, we pass through the door on the left to the Path of Shin שׁ. This is the path of Fire, in a way, even more harrowing than the path of Saturn. In the Tarot, it represents the Last Judgment or, alternatively, the Æon in Thelemic terms.

From the Tarot Trumps:

Here in Fire, we are shown the cosmic forces concentrating on the pilgram from all sides. Judgment is pronounced upon him. He is not the judge nor does decision rest in his hands. Lazarus cannot emerge from the Sepulchre until the voice cries out, "Come forth!" Nor can he cast aside the conflicting grave-clothes until the command, "Loose him!" is given. Man of himself is helpless. The impulse to ascend must come from above, but by its power he may transcend the sepulchre of environment and cast aside the rammels of desire. Here once more, the fiery energy of red burns through the planes. Fiery scarlet, glowing crimson, burning red are emphasized by the passive greens.

From the Thirty-two Paths of Wisdom:

The Thirty-first Path is the Perpetual Intelligence; but why is it so called? Because it regulates the motions of the Sun and Moon in their proper order, each in an orbit convenient for it.

The Path of Resh - ר

Before we enter the Temple or Hod, we must master both paths that lead to it. This means, in addition to the path or Shin, we also must also traverse the path of Resh: ר. Resh, like Shin, is a fiery path. However, while Shin is more primal and elemental, Resh is the Sun, both in its planetary attribution and in the card that represents it.

From the Tarot Trumps:

> *The Watery Paths of trial and probation are counterbalanced by the fiery paths of Temptation, Judgment, and Decision. In violent contrast to the sombre colouring of Aquarius (referring to the path of Tzaddi) and Pisces (Qoph), we are confronted by the flaring hues of the Sun (Resh) and Fire (Shin). The too-aspiring Icarus may find his waxen wings of Ambition and Curiosity shrivelled and melted by the fiery rays of the Sun and the heat of Fire, but approached with humility and reverence, the Sun becomes the beneficent source of life.*
>
> *Protected by an enclosing wall, standing by the Waters of repentance, the Pilgram may submit himself humbly but without fear to the searching Light and absorb warmth and vitality from it for the struggle before him. The colors are clear-orange, golden-yellow, amber shot with red, and the contrasting blue and purple.*

As always, we begin in the Temple of Malkhut. This time we make our way up the middle path of Tav as before, to the Temple of Yesod. Here again are three paths. On the left is Resh, ר. On the right is Tzaddi: צ. In the middle is Samekh: ס. You'll recall we discussed Samekh in the chapter on Tarot as the Temperance card. This is the straight and middle path up the tree that would take you to Tipharet where you meet your Holy Guardian Angel. But we're not ready for that yet. Today we will take the path of Resh to the left.

From the Thirty-two Paths of Wisdom:

The Thirtieth Path is the Collecting Intelligence, and is so called because Astrologers deduce from it the judgment of the stars and celestial signs, and the perfections of their science, according to the rules of the motions of the stars.

The Temple of Hod

Having passed through the fiery trials of Shin and Resh and through humility have gratefully received the beneficent light of the Sun, we are now ready to step into the temple of Hod. As before, the key to this sephirot is the name of God associated with it: *Elohim Tzabaot*. Hod corresponds with the planet Mercury, the number 8, water and knowledge. Here you are likely to meet the archangel Michael.

From Westcott:

The Eighth Path is called the Absolute or Perfect Intelligence, because it is the mean of the primordial, which has no root by which it can cleave, nor rest, except in the hidden places of Gedulah, Magnificence, from which emanates its own proper essence.

The Path of Qoph - ק

We begin again at the temple of Malkhut. By now we have traversed the 32nd path of Tav and the 31st path of Shin (not to mention the 30th path of Resh). We are now prepared to traverse the 29th path of Qoph ק.

From the Tarot Trumps:

> *Here also is a river (referring to the river in the Star card—recall that all the rivers in the Tarot flow from the dress of the High Priestess) but it is the troubled waters of Night, wherein is to be described a crayfish, counterpart of the Scarabeus. From the water's edge winds the dark path of toil, effort and possible failure. It is guarded by the threatening watchdogs, seeking to intimidate the wayfarers, while in the distance the barren hills are surmounted by the frowning fortresses still further guarding the way to attainment. It is the path of blood and tears in which fear, weakness, and fluctuation must be overcome. The colours are dark crimson, reddish brown, brownish crimson and plum colours — but their sombre hues are lightened by the translucent faint greens and yellows to be found in their counterparts.*

From the Thirty-two Paths of Wisdom:

> *The Twenty-ninth Path is the Corporeal Intelligence, so called because it forms every body which is formed in all the worlds, and the reproduction of them.*

The Path of Tzaddi - צ

By this point you should have a sense of how this works. To reach the path of Tzaddi, you must first traverse the path of Tav, as before, to the temple of Yesod. From there, you will take the path on the right, the path of Tzaddi: צ. The path of Tzaddi will have a very different flavor whether you are using the traditional Golden Dawn association with the Star and Aquarius versus Crowley's attribution of it to the Emperor and Aries. In either case, Tzaddi represents the 28th path.

From the Thirty-two Paths of Wisdom:

> *The Twenty-eighth Path is called the Natural Intelligence; by it is completed and perfected the nature of all that exists beneath the sun.*

The Path of Peh - פ

This is the first of the Inner Gateway paths alluded to in the chapter on Tarot. It corresponds with Mars and the Tower card. It is the last path that must be crossed before entering the temple of Netzach, meaning Victory.

The Temple of Netzach and beyond

Netzach is the highest sephirot below Tipharet. There are three paths leading up to Tipharet. These form the veil of Paroket which separates the lower four sephirot from Tipharet and the other sephirot above it. These paths, along with Peh, are what I described as the Inner Gateway in the chapter on Tarot above. Once you have mastered the temple of Netzach, you are ready to approach the paths of Ayin (the Devil), Nun (Death), and finally Samekh (Temperance or Art). While you should walk the paths of Ayin and Nun before approaching Samekh (in order that you may triumph over illusion and fear before walking the middle path between them) it is equally important that your first entrance into the temple of Tipharet be by the path of Samekh. Thus, as you did with the paths of Shin and Qoph the first time you walked them, you will turn back before entering the temple at the other end.

You may find that you approach the temple of Tipharet by the path of Samekh more than once before you feel ready to enter. Tipharet is related to an altogether higher and more universal consciousness than you are typically familiar with. It is also possible you may enter the temple of Tipharet prematurely in which case your vision of it (as with all the paths, actually) will be limited by what you are ready to perceive at that moment. Entering the temple of Tipharet is traditionally associated with entering the Inner Order. Since Tipharet is associated with your Holy Guardian Angel or Daimon, reaching this point may mean that you are ready to undertake the next operation. Note that Pathworking your way up to Tipharet is not a necessary prerequisite for Knowledge and Conversation with your Holy Guardian Angel, nor does it necessarily mean that you are ready for that operation. But it is good practice and will prepare you for that.

Beyond the Veil

Arguably, the most important Magickal operation you will undertake is achieving Knowledge and Conversation with your Holy Guardian Angel or Daimon. This operation was traditionally done by Adepts of the Inner Order. Arguably, success in this operation is a surer sign of true Adepthood than any external initiation rite or ceremony or degree bestowed by any Order. That said, some understanding of the symbolism associated with Adepthood is a good place to start.

Adeptus Minor

In a previous chapter, we discussed how the Order of the Golden Dawn in the Outer was really just preparatory for the Inner Order known as the R.R. et A.C. The first grade in this Inner Order (and arguably the only one that really matters) is Adeptus Minor, or 5=6. This is the grade in which the aspirant is initiated into the sephira of Tipharet, at the heart of the Tree of Life. This sephira is associated with the Sun and with solar deities, including (but not limited to) Christ. The idea of Christ can be interpreted in many ways. One thing we learn from traditional Christian doctrine is that Christ was both human and divine. In Christian orthodoxy, there was only one Christ, supposedly born in Bethlehem about two thousand years ago. However, what we learn from Rosicrucian theology is that we can all be like Christ. To put it another way: we are all capable of becoming demi-gods. How do we do this?

The Book of Abramelin

Sometime around the turn of the 14th century, a man named Abraham of Worms, Germany, wrote a book for his son teaching a method for obtaining Knowledge and Conversation with one's Holy Guardian Angel. He obtained this method from a mage named Abramelin, hence, "the Book of Abramelin." In 1897, Mathers translated *the Book of the Sacred Magic of Abramelin the Mage*. While it was not part of the official curriculum of either the Golden Dawn or the R.R. et A.C, this operation became the *de facto* goal of Adepthood. One might even say that one was not truly an Adept (even if they had received the 5=6 initiation) until they had attained this. I might even go so far as to say that Knowledge and Conversation is *the* distinctive characteristic of the Adept—in some form or another—and not whatever grade you may or may not have received in any Order.

What is the Holy Guardian Angel (or Daimon)?

What is a Holy Guardian Angel, anyway? There are many theories. For the most part, I'd say these theories can be a source of speculative entertainment—of the kind where theologians discuss how many angels can dance on the head of a pin—and at worst, a horrible distraction. One might ask, is your Holy Guardian Angel even real? I have met many magicians—most of whom are not Adepts—state with absolute certainty and confidence that spirits, gods, whatever, are as real as any physical object. One thing I've noticed about the Adepts I've met, however, is that they don't seem to harbor such certainty. If they speak on the subject at all, it tends to be more about their experience, than on any speculation about ultimate reality. However, what I think we would all agree on is that you'd better act *as if* it is real if you hope to have much success. (That said, I've also seen cases where one went into this very skeptical, sure it was all in his imagination, and then something happened that convinced him that his previous conception was far too limited.)

So, let's suppose it is "real", whatever that means. That still doesn't explain what it actually *is*. I don't think it is possible to answer that question, at least not without some particular and unlikely advances in neuropsychology. For a history of the evolution of the concept, I recommend *Holy Daimon* by Frater Acher. This is, to my knowledge, the best book on the subject, both from a historical point of view and (more importantly) from a practical point of view. In this chapter we will only scratch the surface of how to contact your Holy Daimon or Guardian Angel. But in short, this notion of a holy ally has appeared in many cultures, in different forms, across the centuries. Different cultures have had sometimes conflicting things to say about it, though they do all seem to point to the same essential concept. Holy Guardian Angel is the term most often encountered in the context of the Golden Dawn thanks to Mathers' translation of the Book of Abramelin. However, Daimon seems to be the older and more universal term and is the one that I prefer.

There are a few qualities we might want to consider. First: your angel (or daimon) is *yours*. It is not one of the angels we've already been introduced to (though it may take that form). Cat Rose Neligan, in her book *Discovering Your Personal Daimon*, enumerates four faces of the Daimon based upon her comparative research: the Creative Face, the Animal Face, the Divine Face, and the Dark Face. Without going into detail on each of these faces, suffice it to say that your Daimon may appear in many forms and this form may change over time. Given that we are working within the context of Ceremonial Magick, we are most likely to encounter our Daimon with the Divine Face (*i.e.* as an angel). If we were working in a Shamanic context, the Animal Face may be more likely.

Knowledge and Conversation

So now that we have an (albeit vague) sense of what the Holy Guardian Angel or Daimon is, what is Knowledge and Conversation? If the definition of the Daimon is vague, the definition of Knowledge and Conversation is vaguer still. But I will say that it involves a definite sense of encounter with an intelligence that is not your own, and (at least temporarily) two-way communication with it. The more important question is: how do we achieve this?

The Abramelin Operation

When I was a Neophyte, I picked up a book called *21st Century Mage*, by Jason Augustus Newcomb, which had recently been published. It aimed to be a modern update to the 600-year-old classic *Book of Abramelin*. In it, he outlined not only the operation as described in Abraham's book (by way of Mathers' translation) but also a variety of alternatives. All of them involved a sustained Magickal practice that increased in intensity over the duration of months. At the time, I was discouraged from undertaking such an operation so early in my career. Instead, I ended up doing something equally ambitious—to make contact with one of the Tantric Mahavidya—and failed utterly. Why did I fail? My psychic skills were not yet developed. I had read a lot and considered myself rich with knowledge. What I did not realize was that I was still quite poor in understanding. My thoughts on Magick were not my own but were just an intellectual synthesis of what I had read. I had many expectations about how it should work based on what I had read and when my experiences did not meet my expectations, I felt like a failure. My expectations outstripped my abilities.

That said, perhaps my experience would have been different if I had actually followed the original instructions in the *Book of Abramelin*. In the original manuscript, the operation is meant to take a full 18 months of relative solitude and frequent prayer. Needless to say, this is difficult for most people to commit to. I think it is conceivable that a beginner could achieve success with this method on the off chance that they were able to follow it fully. The book was, in fact, intended for someone with no prior Magickal experience.

One of the versions Newcomb includes is one received by Crowley which he described in *The Vision & the Voice*. This version is very similar to the Abramelin Operation except that it takes only 12 weeks. I believe it is assumed that, in this case, the aspirant would already have a considerable amount of experience. The approach described by Frater Acher in *Holy Daimon* takes just four weeks. Like Acher, I was also successful within the span of a month, but I will say that this was after 12 years of experience with the Golden Dawn system of Magick.

Learn to Forget

In a way, everything that I have said in this book up to this point is merely preparatory. Once you are ready to make the leap to contact your Holy Daimon, you will need to forget everything you know about Qabalah, the paths, the Tarot, and so on. By this point, you should have worked with it enough that it is in you. Your knowledge should not be theoretical but based on experience. If you are still looking up correspondences, you may not be ready for this task. (Note: That doesn't mean that you've memorized all the correspondences. Rather, it means that you've developed your intuition to the point that you no longer need them.)

Now you need to be prepared to forget all that, because the fact is, all of this was developed with the intellect—albeit some very impressive intellects—over millennia; but in the end, it is all limited to what can be conceived within the intellect. Where you are going is beyond that. It is more nuanced, and the rules are not as consistent. Things may appear to be their opposite, or at least, the opposite of what you'd expect. Symbolically, you are reaching for the Sun. That is how it occurred to me, but that doesn't mean this will be how you experience it.

Shadow Work

The other thing you will need to do to have any real success with this operation is to deal with your Shadow. The Shadow is another Jungian concept. It is a particular aspect of the unconscious that includes all the things you don't want to deal with or were taught not to deal with. An example I heard is of someone who was always told, "we don't get angry," as a child and so suppressed her anger. She was not allowed to feel her anger, and so her anger, and the things that cause her to be angry, went into her shadow. This can actually be very dangerous because when this person does get angry, they won't know how to deal with it. They may not even realize they are angry! The old saying, "boys don't cry," is another example. Feelings of sadness and vulnerability exist in the Shadow of many who were raised as boys in this culture. But it's not just feelings of sadness or anger that may exist in the Shadow. Pay attention to things about other people that particularly aggravate you, particularly if they seem to bother you more than they bother other people. It could be (not necessarily, but it could be) that this person is acting out something that is reflected in your Shadow. That is, it could be that they are reflecting some aspect of yourself that you would rather not deal with. It is valuable to engage with this prior to attempting to achieve knowledge and conversation with your Daimon. Otherwise, your experience will likely be distorted by your Shadow. One way that you might do this is to personify an aspect of your Shadow as a kind of demon and engage in conversation with it. First, ask it what it wants. Acknowledge that, then ask it what it needs. (You may be surprised by the answer.) Then feed it your love, knowing that you have an endless supply of love to give and that it will be satisfied. If you are worried about feeling drained, draw the love not from within yourself, but from your higher self, your Daimon, who, through the sephira of Tipharet, has the boundless love of deity to impart. A good book on this subject is *Feeding Your Demons*, by Lama Tsultrim Allione. Her approach comes from the Tibetan Chöd practice, but has been adapted to a Western secular context and works well with this approach.

Another way your Shadow might appear is in dreams, particularly nightmares or other dreams that upset you. If you are able to become lucid, then you can engage with your Shadow directly in the dream, which can be very effective. But if not, then simply perform the active imagination exercise described above. That is, in your dream journal, engage in a dialogue with the entity in the dream that upset you. Ask it what it wants. Ask it what it needs. Accept it and feed it love. You may find that it gives you a gift or becomes an ally.

The Bornless Ritual

There is one ritual which many people have found helpful in connecting with their Holy Daimon. While I haven't used it for that purpose, I can attest to the fact that it is very powerful. You'll recall in the Introduction I mentioned the Greek Magical Papyri or PGM. In it is contained a ritual called the Headless One, which Mathers translated as Bornless. Like the Book of Abramelin, the Bornless Ritual, though having no connection to the Golden Dawn system of Magick, became popular among the Adepts of the Order. A complete reproduction of the ritual can be found in the Appendix. Unlike the rituals discussed in Part I, I make no attempt to explain or interpret this ritual. Crowley has done so, though his interpretation is dubious, and unlike with the Golden Dawn rituals, I do not believe an analysis adds anything to the ritual. It is better to take it for what it is: an ancient artifact of immense power.

Practical Magick

High Magick vs. Low Magick

In the beginning of Part II, I discussed how the purpose of the Golden Dawn system of Magick is "to become more than human." I described how that journey takes us beyond the imaginal and puts us in contact with intelligences beyond our own. This, I referred to as "High Magick" while working to cause change in the material world is sometimes referred to as "Low Magick."

People take up Magick for many reasons. Sometimes it comes from a sense that there is something more out there, and they see Magick as a way to reach that. Many others desire power. (And, of course, many are motivated by both.) The idea of Magickal power is very alluring and the idea of "causing change to occur in conformity with will" is attractive indeed. This is, after all, the very definition of Magick, at least according to Aleister Crowley (and many others). However, Crowley did something funny when he gave this definition. He capitalized two words: Change and Will. So the actual definition is this: "Magick is the Science and Art of causing Change to occur in conformity with Will." The key word, however, is not "Change" but "Will", which is the very name of his religion—*Thelema*, in Greek, means Will, which is to be understood as something more primordial than mere desire. An alcoholic in recovery may desire alcohol, but it is their Will to liberate themselves from addiction. To do so is a Magickal act under this definition.

The trick is to know your Will. This is why the chapter on practical Magick follows the one on Inner Work. This is why the chapter on magical squares occurs at the end of the Book of Abramelin, only to be used *after* you have attained Knowledge and Conversation with your Holy Guardian Angel. This is why practical Magick was not taught in the Order of the Golden Dawn in the Outer and was reserved for the Adepts of the R.R. et A.C. That's not to say that you need to be an Adept to engage in practical Magick, but that it is ill advised. Oscar Wilde once said, "When the gods wish to punish us they answer our prayers." In other words, be careful what you wish for.

Invoking Deity and Divining the Outcome

Before engaging in practical Magick, it is good to consult a deeper wisdom than your own. This is one of the reasons why divination is so important to the Magician. The fact is, your conscious mind is simply incapable of taking in all the details, incapable of fully understanding why things are happening the way they are, much less what the effect of casting a spell might actually be in the grand scheme of things. This is usually fine when operating at a normal mundane level, but when taking an action that is likely to significantly affect the outcome of a situation, it is always good to do two things:

1. Invoke the blessings of a higher power.
2. Ask for guidance and to see if what you have in mind is actually a good idea or not.

If you do not do these two things, it is likely that your work will have no effect. That's usually the better outcome. The worse is when it does take effect, but it ends up making the situation worse. (Recall the Wilde quote above.)

Doing the Work

Using Magick to affect the outcome of a situation is all fine and good, but if you don't do the work to make it happen, then nothing will happen. There's a parable I once heard of a pious man living in a house where a hurricane hit. He started praying to his god. A truck came by, and someone yelled out, "Hey, you've got to get out of here! The hurricane is coming!" He replied, "I have faith that my Lord will save me. Go on without me." So, the driver shrugged her shoulders and left. The place started to flood and the man had to go to his roof. He kept praying. A boat came by and said, "Hey, come on! We need to get you out of here!" He replied, "My faith is in God, leave me be. He will deliver me." The boat left and the waters rose further. Finally, a helicopter came by, but he dismissed it as before. The waters rose further and he drowned. When he met his maker, he asked, "Why didn't you save me?" To which his god replied, "What are you talking about? I sent a truck, a boat, and a helicopter! It's not my fault you were too stupid to get in."

Many writings on Magick say that what Magick does is that it alters the "probability field" or something like that. It's a pseudo-scientific explanation, but it's as good as any you're likely to get. Magick by itself will not get you a job; but if you do the work, prepare your resume, apply for the jobs you want, and put your best foot forward, Magick may help. Is Magick actually making a change in the outside world, or are you just allowing it to change you into someone more capable of getting that job? It is difficult to know. And in the end, if your goal is to get the job, it doesn't really matter, does it?

Picking a Focus

To work this kind of Magick, you need some kind of focus. Usually what you want can be attributed to one of the seven planets discussed in the ritual of the Hexagram. Other effective foci could be a Tarot card—for example, Three of Cups to promote harmony in a group—or a Geomantic figure—such as Acquisitio to gain something.

> ### PLANETS AND GODS
>
> In the section above I alluded to the importance of invoking deity. It's perhaps worthwhile to comment on the relationship between the planets and gods, especially since the planets are named after gods. This is an important point: the planets are named after gods, not the other way around. The planet Mars, associated with Gevurah on the Qabalistic Tree, is not the same as the god Mars. The planet Mars is like a kind of energy or power or quality. It may have a personality, but it is not a person. Gods, on the other hand, are complex, multifaceted beings,

much more like a person than an energy. You would not invoke the planet Mars for love, but you might invoke the god Mars, particularly if you already had a good relationship with him. I mention this because I personally found it confusing when I saw hymns to various gods that seemed to go far beyond the qualities I associated with them based on their little box on the Tree of Life. I did not realize at the time that this kind of thinking was incredibly reductive and even offensive, as though, once knowing someone's astrological sun sign, you think you know all about them. The difference being, of course, that we are influenced by the zodiac, but it is the zodiac that gets its names and attributions from the gods.

Do not try to build a relationship with every god. Do try to build a relationship with every planet. Whatever god or angel or spirit becomes your tutor or guide, they can help you work with all the planets and powers. You do not need to have a shrine to Aries to cast a Mars spell.

Putting it to Work

Once you've got your focus, you are ready to get to work. The traditional Golden Dawn approach to practical Magick is to effectively "initiate" your talisman as though it were a Neophyte in the Golden Dawn. It is an incredibly complicated process; I might even say over-complicated. The formula I will describe is much simpler, though still somewhat more complicated then you might get in a book on witchcraft. (This is a book on ceremonial Magick, after all.) Basically, it consists of four steps:

1. Cleansing the Space (LBRP & BRH)
2. Empowering the Space (SIRP & optional MP)
3. Invoking the Power (IRH & optional MP)
4. Cleaning up Afterward (optional BRH & LBRP)

Cleansing the Space

The banishing rituals of the pentagram and hexagram have already been described to you. Before you engage in any practical Magick, you should have these thoroughly memorized. If you have not had enough experience with these two rituals to be able to do them effectively by heart, you are unlikely to have much success with what follows.

Empowering the Space

Here I put SIRP and optional MP. SIRP stands for Supreme Invoking Ritual of the Pentagram. You might recall that in the chapter on the Ritual of the Pentagram I made mention of the ritual "in its supreme form". Well, that's what we're going to get into here. As for MP, that stands for Middle Pillar. You'll note that I included "optional MP" for both Empowering the Space and Invoking the Power. They are different. For Empowering the Space, I recommend doing the traditional Middle Pillar exercise, empowering your aura with the names of God associated with the sephirot along the middle pillar from *Eheieh Asher Eheieh* to *Adonai ha-Aretz*. The Middle Pillar used in Invoking the Power is different and I will get to that below.

Supreme Invoking Ritual of the Pentagram

The Supreme or Greater Ritual of the Pentagram follows the same pattern as the Lesser with a more elaborate step 2: formulation of the Pentagrams. The rest is exactly as before. As a recap, the four steps are:

1. The Qabalistic Cross
2. Formulation of the Pentagrams
3. Evocation of the Archangels
4. The Qabalistic Cross (again)

By now, the Qabalistic Cross and Evocation of the Archangels should be very familiar to you, so I won't repeat those. You'll recall, in the Lesser or Simple ritual, you used just one Pentagram (typically the banishing Pentagram of Earth) and these four names: YHVH, Adonai, Eheieh, and AGLA. To these we will add two more Hebrew God-names—Elohim and EL—as well as eight names in Enochian.

> **WHAT THE HECK IS ENOCHIAN?**
>
> A full description of the language of Enochian is outside the scope of this book, but to the student of ceremonial Magick, it is likely to come up. Since there is so much misinformation out there about this strange language, it seems appropriate to provide a little context. First, the term "Enochian" refers to the Biblical patriarch Enoch who is said to have lived prior to the Flood, and prior to the Tower of Babel. This means that he is said to have spoken the original language, or the language of Adam, prior to the separation of human speech into many languages. This language is said to have had incredible Magickal power, even greater than Hebrew, which was considered a corrupted form of this proto-language, though the closest to the original that we had ... at least until the work of John Dee and Edward Kelley. In the late 1500s, these two Englishmen in Poland undertook an incredible magickal experiment to contact what they believed to be angels. Through Edward Kelley, these angels revealed several names and "calls" in the form of apocalyptic verse in an unknown language. They believed this to be the language of the angels, which would also have been the language of Adam and Enoch in its uncorrupted form (so they believed). Though Dee and Kelley never referred to this language as "Enochian" (but rather "Angelic"), that was what the founders of the Golden Dawn called it, and the name stuck. If you are interested in exploring this further, I recommend the book *Enochian Vision Magick* by Lon Milo DuQuette. There are many other books as well, of varying quality, but that is the only one I could recommend without qualification.

We will also enhance our Pentagrams with symbols drawn in the center to further activate and distinguish them. First are the spirit Pentagrams. These come in two flavors: active and passive. Active is used in the East and South for the active elements of Air and Fire. Passive is used in the West and North for the passive elements of Water and Earth. The invoking active Pentagrams are drawn from going from the lower active element (Fire–lower right) to the upper active element (Air–upper left). The invoking passive Pentagrams are drawn from going from the lower passive element (Earth–lower left) to the upper passive element (Water–upper right). This is followed by tracing a spirit wheel in the center of the Pentagram. The spirit wheel is simply a circle with eight spokes:

Element	Symbol	Hebrew	Pentagram	Enochian	Direction
Spirit (Active)	Wheel	Eheieh	bottom right to top left	Exarp	East
				Bitom	South
Spirit (Passive)		AGLA	bottom left to top right	Hcoma	West
				Nanta	North

During the tracing of the Pentagram, vibrate the Enochian Spirit name of the element you are facing. So, Exarp for Air in the East. Bitom for Fire in the South. Hcoma for Water in the West. Nanta for Earth in the North. During the tracing of the spirit wheel, vibrate the Hebrew name associated with active or passive spirit. So that's Eheieh in the East and South; Agla in the West and North.

After you formulate the pentagram of active spirit in the East, you will formulate the invoking pentagram or Air in the East. This you will do by tracing across to the point of Air from the upper right to the upper left, then down and so on. As you do this, vibrate the three Enochian names of God associated with the East. They are: Oro, Ibah, Aozpi. Then trace the sign of Aquarius in the center of the pentagram ♒, and vibrate the Hebrew name of God associated with Air, which is the Tetragrammaton, Yod-Heh-Vav-He.

Element	Symbol	Hebrew	Pentagram	Enochian	Direction
Air	Aquarius ♒	YHVH	top right to top left	Oro Ibah Aozpi	East
Fire	Leo ♌	Elohim	top to bottom right	Oip Teaa Pdoce	South
Water	Eagle 🦅	El	top left to top right	Empeh Arsel Gaiol	West
Earth	Taurus ♉	AGLA	top to bottom left	Mor Dial Hctga	North

You then proceed to the South, perform the invoking pentagram of Spirit Active again, but this time with the name Bitom and conclude with the invoking pentagram of Fire, with Leo in the center, and so on. Here's the outline:

1. Go to the East. Make the invoking Pentagram for Spirit Active, visualized in white light. Vibrate EXARP while drawing the Pentagram. Draw the wheel within the Pentagram. Vibrate EHEIEH while making the wheel.

2. Make the invoking Pentagram of Air, visualized in yellow light. Vibrate ORO IBAH AOZPI while drawing the Pentagram. Draw the Aquarius symbol (♒) within the Pentagram. Vibrate YHVH while making this symbol.

3. Trace the circle clockwise to South. Make the invoking Pentagram for Spirit Active, visualized in white light. Vibrate BITOM while drawing the Pentagram. Draw the wheel within the Pentagram. Vibrate EHEIEH while making the wheel.

4. Make the invoking Pentagram of Fire, visualized in red light. Vibrate OIP TEAA PEDOCE while drawing the Pentagram. Draw the Leo symbol (♌) within the Pentagram. Vibrate ELOHIM while making this symbol.

5. Trace the circle clockwise to West. Make the invoking Pentagram for Spirit Passive, visualized in white light. Vibrate HCOMA while drawing the Pentagram. Draw the wheel within the Pentagram. Vibrate AGLA while making the wheel.
6. Make the invoking Pentagram of Water, visualized in blue light. Vibrate EMPEH ARSEL GAIOL while drawing the Pentagram. Draw the head of the eagle (🦅) within the Pentagram. Vibrate EL while making this symbol.
7. Trace circle clockwise to the North. Make the invoking Pentagram for Spirit Passive, visualized in white light. Vibrate NANTA while drawing the Pentagram. Draw the wheel within the Pentagram. Vibrate AGLA while making the wheel.
8. Make the invoking Pentagram of Earth, visualized in green light. Vibrate EMOR DIAL HECTEGA while drawing the Pentagram. Draw the Taurus symbol (♉) within the Pentagram. Vibrate ADONAI while making this symbol.

The symbols for Air and Water might be confusing. The symbol for Air, ♒, looks like water. It is, however, the symbol for Aquarius, the fixed sign of Air. The symbol for water is similarly confusing in that it is the head of an Eagle, 🦅. One might assume that the symbol of a bird would be associated with Air, but no. In this case it is associated with the *kerub* of Water, and therefore goes in the West.

You'll notice how this compares to the Lesser or Simple ritual. In that case, we used four four-letter names of God, utilizing the two names associated with active and passive spirit, respectively, and for the other two, utilizing the names associated with Air and Earth. Air being an Active element and Earth being a passive element, this formed an Active axis from East to West (YHVH-Eheieh) and a Passive axis from South to North (Adonai-AGLA). The Lesser ritual is, in a way, a compressed form of the Supreme ritual.

After invoking Earth in the North, return to center, and finish as before, evoking the archangels and finishing with the Qabalistic Cross. As an alternative, the Bornless Ritual can also work for this step.

Invoking the Power

Now that the space has been fully opened, it is time to get specific and draw upon the energy you have in mind. More likely than not, there is a particular planet that rules this operation, so we will go with that assumption. Here you will perform the Invoking Ritual of the Hexagram (IRH) for that planet. Optionally, you may wish to follow that up with a Middle Pillar, but this time using the Godname associated with the sephirah associated with that planet. So, for example, if you are working with Hod, you would invoke the name *Elohim Tzabaoth*. You don't need to do both Middle Pillars.

Invoking Ritual of the Hexagram

The Invoking Ritual of the Hexagram of a given planet is similar to the Ritual of the Hexagram provided above with the difference that instead of banishing the celestial elements through their respective Hexagrams of fire, earth, air and water; we will instead be using the invoking hexagram of the planet in question. The

Hexagram of each planet is determined by its corresponding sephirah in the Qabalistic Tree with the Sun in Tipharet at the center. The Moon, corresponding to Yesod, is at the bottom-most point. Mercury, corresponding with Hod, is in the bottom-left. Venus, corresponding with Netzach, is in the lower-right. Mars, corresponding with Gevurah, is in the upper-left. Jupiter, corresponding with Chesed, is in the upper-right. Finally, Saturn, corresponding with Binah is (like in the Middle Pillar exercise) displaced to Da'at and thus at the top of the Hexagram. Hexagrams are drawn with two triangles as before, starting with the point of the planet you are working with. So, if you are invoking

Mercury, you start with the lower left point and then draw the second triangle starting from the opposing angle in the upper right. If you are invoking Saturn, you start at the top and then draw the second triangle starting from the bottom.

(Note again that the hexagram of Saturn and the hexagram of Earth are the same, again alluding to the connection between Binah and Malkhut.) When invoking, you go clockwise. When banishing, counter-clockwise.

You will then trace the symbol of the planet within the center of the hexagram. During the tracing of the hexagram, you will vibrate ARARITA as before. While drawing the symbol of the planet, vibrate the God-name associated with the sephirah associated with that planet. *Shaddai El-Chai* for the Moon, for instance.

> When invoking the moon, you will almost certainly want to invoke it in its waxing aspect. So, trace the sign thus: ☽ The waning sign (☾) should only be used in cases of restriction or destruction.

Should you want to invoke the sun, you will trace all six hexagrams, intoning ARARITA each time. Then finally draw sign of the sun ☉ in the center and vibrate YHVH Eloah ve-Da'at. As usual, open and close with the Analysis of the Keyword.

Charging a Talisman

Depending on the operation, it may also make sense to use the planetary hexagram to charge a talisman or other object. Here you formulate the hexagram as before, with this difference: after drawing the hexagram, before drawing the sign, draw a circle around the hexagram to contain its power within your focus.

Cleaning up Afterward

Once you are done, you will want to clean up your temple. Even if the power you are working with is wholly beneficent, once you have completed the operation, it is always good to return to a baseline. You do this by performing the Banishing Ritual of the Hexagram (BRH) followed by the Lesser Banishing Ritual of the Pentagram (LBRP). It is also always a good idea to eat something after this if at all possible. It is also a good idea to pay particular attention to your dreams after such an operation to see if anything shows up.

Note about Goetia

In the above operation, we discussed harnessing planetary powers in order to assist in achieving a certain outcome. This is, of course, just one of many (many!) ways of performing practical Magick. It is, for the most part, safe (particularly if you banish afterwards). The biggest risk is if you do not banish afterwards, you may suffer some mental imbalance due to the planetary influence. Everything in this operation is overseen by the divine Will and so it is unlikely anything will go terribly wrong.

Now, some people like a more personal touch with their Magick. And by that, I mean a touch of a person, particularly of the non-human variety. These come in many flavors. We've spent some time discussing angels, and these, again, for the most part, are safe. Some angels (like Samael) are not necessarily very fond of humans, but they will not really harm you. They do not have free will.

But what about beings that do have free will? What about faeries, djinn, and demons? What about Goetia? What is Goetia, anyway? Well, to begin with, it is one of the more popular grimoires that is part of the Lesser Key of Solomon. It describes 72 beings that can be engaged to perform any number of tasks. Some of them appear to be related to Pagan gods that have, through the conquering of monotheistic faiths, been transformed into malevolent spirits. (The most notable of these being the 29th spirit, AsTaroth, who was once the goddess Astarte.) Here's the problem: the Goetia was written within a Judeo-Christian context in which all spirits that were not considered a part of the kingdom of heaven were considered, by definition, evil, and were to be treated with extreme prejudice and even brutality. The Goetia consists of numerous methods of torturing these beings to get them to comply with your wishes. This is not how I choose to engage with the spirit world, and it is not how I would teach someone else to do so either.

There is, however, another way. The fact is, the term Goetia was not invented by Jewish or Christian magicians but is rather rooted in an old pagan Grecian tradition which held a much more respectful relationship with these earthly spirits. I don't believe anyone ever took them to be particularly benevolent, but that doesn't mean they were particularly malevolent either—that is, unless you offend them, which is what often happens during forced conversion. If you wish to engage with such beings, particularly if you consider yourself a Pagan (but even if you don't, and simply want to have a more respectful relationship with the spirit world) I recommend you approach them as a Pagan would. Do not bind them. Do not torture them. Invite them to you. Offer them gifts, but always keep your guard up. Remember to use the Pentagram should you feel threatened; it will protect you.

The same goes for faeries, elves, and other nature spirits. (It is an open question as to whether these are truly different species, or whether the differences between them say more about the culture describing them than about the beings themselves. I'm inclined toward the latter, but I don't really know.) If the Goetia appeal to you, I strongly recommend the writings of Jake Stratton-Kent and those he influenced, such as Frater Acher and (to a lesser extent) Peter Grey.

Servitors and Thought-Forms

Another kind of entity you may wish to work with are called servitors or thought-forms. I do not believe these to be fundamentally different from talismans or spells, they have simply been anthropomorphized. This can be advantageous as you can then have a conversation with this being. Unlike Goetia, servitors and thought-forms are created by you.

They do not have their own agenda but exist as an extension of your will.

I've read of people taking this to an extreme and creating a long-lived thought-form known as a *tulpa*. This is a kind of familiar or imaginary friend. I'll admit, this is somewhat outside the realm of my own expertise, but I wanted to mention it. One could make a thought-form using the formula above, imbuing the entity with planetary energy according to its purpose. If I were to make a *tulpa*, it is probably one of the few places where I would want to use the hexagram of the Sun, as this would indirectly grant it access to all the planetary powers and would also keep it balanced. I could even imagine such a being taking on a role not unlike a guardian angel over time. But that is mere speculation on my part.

Part 3:
Conclusion

In this relatively short book, I have attempted to communicate the essentials of the Magickal path gleaned from over twenty years of experience, following it, abandoning it, picking it up again, walking away from it again, and returning to it once more. While this book is considerably shorter than many other introductions to Magick, it contains with it all you really need to know to use this system to transform your life. If you have read carefully and performed the practices, you now have the grammar of Magick.

What I left out

To keep this book short and focus on what I believe to be essential, there are a number of things I did not include in this book that you might find in a typical introduction to Magick.

Magickal Tools

One of the things this book did not include (which many books on Magick do) is instructions on how to make Magickal tools. This was for two reasons. First, this book was written for people with extremely limited means, and so to provide instructions that required one to get a lathe, molding clay, paints, engraving tools, and so on, would be offensive. But perhaps more importantly: You don't need them. As famed ceremonial magician, Lon Milo DuQuette (one of my very favorite authors and one of the few ceremonial magicians I know with a good sense of humor—I recommend all of his books) put it when describing how to make a Magick Ring out of paper which would traditionally be made out of gold:

> *I realize such material is not as impressive or romantic as pure gold. You might even think that a true magick Ring cannot be made from a scrap of paper. You might tell me you'd feel silly wearing a paper ring. If you feel*

> *this way, then I hope you won't be offended when I tell you that if you can't make a real magick Ring out of paper, then you'll not be able to make one out of gold. The same goes for the other magical items.*

When I perform Ceremonial Magick, the tools I will have, when convenient, include a wand of double power, incense, a cup of water, and an altar. The wand of double power is described in the section of Formulating the Pentagrams in the chapter on the Ritual of the Pentagram. But the fact is, I more often just use my finger.

Water to purify and incense to consecrate are nice, I will say. The water is easy, you just need a cup of water that you can dip three fingers in and sprinkle outward, saying "I purify with water." You can do this around the space that you are working in as well as on any people or objects within that circle. Incense, of course, is less convenient. It may be difficult to get, depending on your circumstances. There may be rules prohibiting fire where you live. There may be smoke and/or scent sensitivities to be concerned about. Neither water nor incense are essential. They are both just nice to have when it's convenient. While they are best used together, you can use one without the other.

The altar is arguably the most important, but even that can be done away with. It is only necessary if you are trying to focus your work on something, say, creating a talisman (in which case you also need the talisman). An altar is just a place set aside for the work. Ideally it should be raised up, but, if necessary, it could just be a clear spot on the floor. The traditional Golden Dawn altar is a double cube, which has important symbolic significance. I still have not bothered to make a double cubical altar. My little side table works fine.

If you do have an altar, it is good to decorate it with objects conducive to the work you are doing, and which do not distract from it. If you have an altar to Thor or Shiva, that should be separate from the altar that you use to create a Mercury talisman. Then again, if you typically invoke Thor or Shiva to bless all your workings, then I see no harm in including them in your Magickal altar. In the end it's just about what feels right to you. The important thing is to tune into that feeling and not let me or anyone else tell you what's right for you.

Elemental Exercises

Another thing I see in some introductions to Magick are elemental exercises: ways of connecting with the Platonic elements of Earth, Air, Water, and Fire. In the context of ceremonial Magick, this corresponds with the four elemental grades of the Order of the Golden Dawn in the Outer. This book does not intend to be a substitute for the elemental grades and so does not try to mimic them. That's not to say that I do not find these exercises useful and effective. I also find the elemental grades themselves to be useful and effective. But they are not essential. I'm not even sure if I would call them ceremonial Magick *per se*. If you wish to spend time working with each element, I certainly encourage you to do so. You can use the invoking Pentagrams of that element and come up with experiments of your own invention to deepen your connection with that element. One thing you might do to get your imagination going would be to start with a mind map like the one I described in the introduction about finding associations with the word Magick, only this time do it for each of the elements. Then try engaging with what comes up. Walking barefoot for Earth. Breathing exercises for Air. Long showers for Water. Candle gazing for Fire.

Walking the Path

It will take a lot longer to master the material in this book than it took you to read it. If this were a correspondence course, I might have padded the material to make sure you give ample time to each exercise before introducing the next one. The fact is that even though this book is short, it contains enough material to be worked on for years. My hope is that if you have found this book interesting and useful enough to reach this point, that you will not abandon it once you have finished reading it, but that you will continue to practice the exercises contained within, exploring their different aspects, working with different elements and planets, meditating on the Geomantic figures, working the paths on the Qabalistic tree, and so on. Even once you've attained Knowledge and Conversation, you are not done. In fact, many would say that's when the work really begins.

Beyond this Book

While I have attempted to cover all the essentials required to follow this path, this little book is by no means exhaustive. There are, of course, many other books one could read, and I will mention some of the more notable ones below. These days, there are also many ephemeral resources that weren't available in the last century, much less those of the Victorian era, such as podcasts and websites. I won't go into too much detail there since those resources change so quickly, and anything I'd recommend would likely be replaced by the time you read this. But perhaps the most important resource is other people.

Groups

Magickal working groups form an important part of this tradition. While it is true that most practitioners are solitary, it is worth remembering that the material in this book was originally developed for a working group. This is actually pretty unusual as Magickal traditions go. While there are stories of covens of witches going back centuries, my sense is that most Magickal knowledge was passed mouth-to-ear, from teacher to student, with the teacher sometimes being a spirit. The Golden Dawn, taking the Masonic Lodge as its prototype, organized itself into temples where a candidate would be initiated by a group of officers—at least three, and preferably seven or more. It is a pity that of the many people who follow this Magickal path, only relatively few get to experience a proper ritual initiation. While ceremonial initiation is in no way necessary in making Magickal progress, it can help. There are two types of groups: big ones and small ones.

Big Groups

There are a few large groups that can trace lineage back to the historical Order of the Golden Dawn, at least one of which actually calls itself the Hermetic Order of the Golden Dawn. I will say, the more I learn about these groups, the more I encounter their members and former members, the more I am glad to have never joined one. Use your own judgment, of course, but I advise you not to be dazzled by claims of historicity. It can be interesting history, like knowing that you are descended from Genghis Khan, but that is all. Just because you have a bit of Gengis Khan's DNA doesn't mean you are a conqueror. It just means that Genghis Khan made a lot of babies.

That said, some of these groups do produce high quality materials. I have heard good things about the Builders of the Adytum's correspondence course. So that might be worth pursuing if you have the means. The Society of Inner Light—the descendant of Dion Fortune's Fraternity of Inner Light—also provides a correspondence course. I have not followed that one, nor do I know anyone who has, but I do know Dion Fortune to be a highly regarded figure in the history of this tradition, and a good author, so I would expect quality. But, as always, exercise your own discretion. Trust your wise self—that is, your Holy Daimon. Listen to your inner voice when encountering groups like this (or anywhere, really) and if that voice says something seems wrong here, listen to it.

One other group worth mentioning is Quareia. It was developed by Josephnie McCarthy with the help of Frater Acher. Frater Acher wrote *Holy Daimon* which I mentioned in Part II. Quareia manages to avoid many of the pitfalls of the large groups by frankly prohibiting them. It also has one large advantage over correspondence courses like that of the B.O.T.A.: it's entirely free. I have not pursued it myself. By the time it was developed, I did not feel like starting over again. But it may be worth pursuing. It's worth noting that Queria is *not* a Golden Dawn-style order. However, it does teach its own form of ceremonial Magick, which from my admittedly brief perusal appears to be largely compatible with what is here.

Small Groups

For every large group, there are probably hundreds of small groups like the one that initiated me. These can be hard to find and tend not to last very long. You might get lucky and find one. Of course, as always, use judgment when approaching these groups. All my warnings about large groups apply as well to small ones. There are plenty of people in either case who will try to use the group to their own self-(lower-case 's')-aggrandizement.

It's perhaps also worth pointing out that every large group is composed of small groups. I've known many members of the Ordo Templi Orientis to wax poetically about some period in their Oasis' history (O.T.O. is organized by Oasis, instead of Lodge or Temple) when things were going just right. Then something happens, people move away, or just get tired, and the Magick is over. It's sometimes sad to hear these stories, but also encouraging, because what happened in the 1970s or 1990s could happen again today.

Starting a Group

If you are not lucky enough to find a group near you, or you find one but it's not a good fit, one other option is to do what my teacher did: start your own. I would say there's essentially two ways to do this: as a peer-group, studying and working together to figure things out as equals; or as a hierarchical Order. The peer-group is relatively safe. The only problem is that it makes it harder for one person to take on the role of Hierophant, which is necessary for the group to really be elevated from just a group of practitioners to a Magickal body in and of itself.

The dangers of a hierarchical Order should be obvious, but I'll spell it out anyway: in short, it can get to the Hierophant's head. To begin with, no one should take on the role of Hierophant until after (at a minimum) they have achieved Knowledge and Conversation with their Holy Daimon. If their Daimon agrees that this is the way to go, one can proceed, but carefully. I won't go too far into this, since I have never done it myself, though I have witnessed what can go wrong when being Hierophant goes to a leader's head (even with and despite the guidance of their Daimon). There is a book about this called *the Work of the Hierophant* by Josephine McCarthy. I recommend it for anyone seriously considering this path. If that book doesn't scare you out of it, you are either ready, or beyond help.

Books

There are far too many books on Magick to discuss here. But there are two essential books worth discussing, plus a few others that I've mentioned along the way. The first is Israel Regardie's *The Golden Dawn*. Originally published in four volumes between 1937 and 1940, it is now on its 7th edition. I have the 6th edition, which is sometimes referred to as "the Black Book" or "the Black Brick" because that's what it looks like, and perhaps that's what it feels like when you try to glean any information out of it. In other words, it is opaque and dense. That said, it is a great resource for both the experienced practitioner with tremendous patience and/or the researcher. Recent editions do have a very good index, which is essential, given that it is not so much a book as a collection of somewhat random papers loosely organized.

There is another book that reproduces the essential Outer Order materials of *The Golden Dawn* but in a more sensible course-like structure. This book is called *Self-Initiation into the Golden Dawn Tradition* by the Ciceros. It is also sometimes referred to as "the Green Book" (in contrast to "the Black Book"). The subtitle is "A Complete Curriculum of Study for Both the Solitary Magician and the Working

Magical Group" but I believe it would require an already fairly advanced practitioner to use it solitary. However, if you do decide to form a group, this book will provide useful instructions on how to do proper initiations including guidelines that are either missing or hidden in the Black Book.

The other somewhat essential book I must mention is *Magick* by Aleister Crowley, also known as Book 4. This book is very dense, but it is at least organized somewhat sensibly. That said, the most useful part of Book 4, in my opinion, are the copious appendices. It's worth noting that a tremendous amount of Crowley's writings, including all of Book 4, can be found for free online at hermetic.com. I'm normally reluctant to recommend websites since they so quickly disappear, but this one has been going strong since 1996, so it seems fair to say it should last a bit longer. Likewise, they can be found on esotericarchives.com and sacred-texts.com, the latter of which is generally not as well formatted as the versions in hermetic.com but has a much wider selection.

One final book on Magick that I must recommend is *Modern Magick* by Donald Michael Kraig. It is now on its third edition. It, along with the Green Book, was my primary guide through the early steps of this path. It is very beginner-friendly and also very complete, and is the only book I know of that is both. When I forget how to do a ritual, that's the book I reach for first. His curriculum of 12 lessons is loosely based on the grades of both the Order of the Golden Dawn in the Outer (consisting of the first six lessons) and the R.R. et A.C. (consisting of the last six lessons). In this it is similar to this book but goes into much greater detail. It's worth noting that Kraig introduced an innovation in his curriculum that was picked up by many smaller Orders, including mine, and that is moving some of the Inner Order material into the preliminary instruction.

Finally, though this book is not connected to the Golden Dawn or Ceremonial Magick in any way, I would like to mention *The Red Book* by Carl Jung. He was a Psychologist in the early 20th century whose ideas have had a profound impact on the Western world. He was deeply interested in alchemy and gnosticism and discovered his own path to contacting his Holy Daimon. It was reading *The Red Book* that inspired me to finally try to achieve Knowledge and Conversation on my own and I did so using his method called Active Imagination. The method of Active Imagination is described fully in Robert Johnson's book, *Inner Work*. Though "Active Imagination" is not a term associated with Ceremonial Magick *per se*, it perfectly describes what I believe to be taking place in path working and spirit work and I believe the Jungian approach to be far easier to grasp than what is described by most Magickal authors, which I generally find more confusing than helpful.

Websites

Websites tend to come and go quickly, and so it is dangerous to recommend any one in particular. The three I mentioned already are worth reiterating: hermetic.com, esotericarchives.com, and sacred-texts.com. They both contain vast resources in the public domain. One more worth mentioning is archive.org which is useful in a number of ways: first is the WayBack Machine. So if you come across a website that no longer exists, you can usually find it there. Second is its collection of books, which is quite extensive. It's worth noting that, in my experience, Google and other search engines rarely produce results including these websites. So, if you search Google for "Aleister Crowley Magick" you will be given a link to where to buy it on Amazon or Barnes & Noble, but not the links to hermetic.com or sacred-texts.com containing the complete text for free.

Your Self

We live in an age of information. Gone are the days in which one group, library, or university could claim special access to knowledge that no one else had. That's not to say that there aren't still secret techniques out there, but even those get leaked periodically (like *the Golden Dawn*), and it becomes clear that there are only so many ways to teach meditation and Magick. The difficult part is navigating the sea of information. I see two parts to this: one is having the basic tools to understand what you're working with. That is what I try to provide in this book. The other is knowing where to go. This is where a curriculum, like Queria, or the B.O.T.A.'s correspondence course, or Kraig's *Modern Magick* are valuable, because you don't have to think about it. You just need to follow the instructions in the next lesson. Sooner or later, though, you run out of instructions. A physicist I knew said the experience of getting a PhD was like taking a bullet train to the edge of the world and then having to get out and walk. Curricula in Magick are perhaps less like bullet trains and more like steam-powered locomotives, but in the end, it's the same: you need to get out and walk. This can be frustrating. The only advice I can give you here is to listen to your inner voice and see where it guides you. You do not need to have achieved Knowledge and Conversation to do that. Your Daimon is already with you, you just need to listen. This is, perhaps, the most important lesson of all. If you can remember to do that, then everything else will flow.

Part 4: Appendices

The Tarot Trumps

The Tarot Trumps, by G.H. Soror Q.L.[3] is a document that was circulated in the original Order of the Golden Dawn. It is one of the earliest descriptions of what the Major Arcana of the Tarot is supposed to look like. Unlike the version commissioned by Arthur Edward Waite (also a member of the Golden Dawn), this version was meant for initiates only. You may notice some differences in the descriptions from the Smith-Waite and other Golden Dawn-influenced decks.

༄ ༅

The cards of the Lesser Arcana present to us the vibrations of Number, Color, and Element—that is, the plane on which number and color function. Thus, in the Ten of Pentacles we have the number Ten tertiary colors, citrine, olive, and russet, working in Malkuth, the material plane. Whereas in the Ten of Wands we have the number Ten and the tertiaries working in pure energy. In these cards, the Sephirah is indicated by the coloring of the clouds; the plane by the coloring of the symbols.

The four honors of each suit taken in their most abstract sense may be interpreted as:

- Potential Power - The King
- Brooding Power - The Queen
- Power in Action - The Prince
- Reception and Transmission - The Princess.

All these cards are colored according to their elements plus the Sephirah to which they are attributed. With the Greater Arcana, the

---

[3] Probably "Greatly Honored Soror Quaero Lucem", the motto of Harriet Miller Davidson according to Giordano Berti.

Trumps, however, we are given the Keys to divine manifestation, each one an individual force to be considered independently. It must never be forgotten that the Trumps are intrinsically, glyphs of cosmic, not human, force.

The Foolish Man

This card as usually presented shows a man in motley striding along, heedless of the dog which tears his garments and threatens to attack him. In this is seen only the lower aspect of the card, giving no hint to the Divine Folly of which St. Paul speaks. But in the Order pack, an effort is made to reveal the deeper meaning. A naked child stands beneath a rose-tree bearing yellow roses—the golden Rose of Joy as well as the Rose of Silence. While reaching up to the Roses, he yet holds in leash a gray wolf, worldly wisdom held in check by perfect innocence. The colors are pale yellow, pale blue, greenish yellow - suggestive of the early dawn of a spring day.

The Magician

It represents the union and balance of the elemental powers controlled by mind. The Adept dedicating the minor implements on the Altar. The apths of Beth and Mercury link Kether toe Crown with Binah, the Aimah Elohim. The Magician, therefore, is reflected in the Intellect which stores and gathers up knowledge and pours it into the House of Life, Binah. The number of the Path, 12, suggests the synthesis of the Zodiac, as Mercury is the synthesis of the planets. The colors yellow, violet, gray, and indigo, point to the mysterious astral light surrounding the great Adept. It is a card lihnked with the name Tahuti and Hermes as the previous one is with Krishna nad Harparkrat or Dionysius.

The High Priestess

The High Priestess rules the long path uniting Kether to Tiphareth, crossing the reciprocal Paths of Venus and Leo. She is the great feminine force controlling the very source of life, gathering into herself all the energizing forces and holding them in solution until the time of release. Her colors, pale blue, deepening into sky blue, silvery white, and silver, relieved by touches of orange and flame, carry out these ideas.

The Empress

She is an aspect of Isis; the creative and positive side of Nature is suggested here. The Egyptian trilogy, Isis, Hathor and Nephthys, symbolized by the crescent, full moon, and gibbous moon are represented in the Tarot by the High Priestess, Hathor. The Empress, Isis, takes either the crescent moon or Venus as her symbol. Justice, Nephthys, takes the gibbous moon.

Isis and Venus gives the aspect of Love, while Hathor is rather the Mystic, the full moon reflecting the Sun of Tiphareth while in Yesod, transmitting the rays of the Sun in her path Gimel. In interpreting a practical Tarot it is often admissible to regard the Empress as standing for Occultism. The High Priestess for religion, the Church as distinguished from the Order.

The Empress, whose letter is Daleth, is the Door of the inner mysteries, as Venus is the door of the Vault. Her colors are emerald, sky-blue, blue-green, and cerise or rose-pink.

The Emperor

Here we have the great energizing forces as indicated by the varying shades of red. It may be noted here that the red paths remain red in all planes, varying only in shade. Thus Aries, the Emperor, the Pioneer, the General, is blood and deep crimson, red, pure vermillion or flowing fiery red. He is Ho Nike, the Conqueror, hot, passionate, impetuous, the apotheosis of Mars, whether in love or in war. He is the positive masculine as the Empress is the positive feminine.

The Hierophant

The High Priest is the counterpart of the High Priestess. As Aries is the house of Mars and the exaltation of the Sun, so Taurus is the house of Venus and the exaltation of the Moon. He is the reflective or mystical aspect of the masculine. He is the thinker as the Emperor is the doer.

His colors, unlike those of the Emperor, vary considerably. Red, orange, maroon, deep brown, and chestnut brown, suggest veiled thought, interior power, endurance, contemplation and reconciliation. This card frequently indicates the hidden guardianship of the Masters.

The Lovers

The impact of inspiration on intuition, resulting in illumination and liberation—the sword striking off the fetters of habit and materialism, Perseus rescuing Andromeda from the Dragon of fear and the waters of stagnation. (Note: Incidentally note that this is the design of the Order card. Andromeda is shown manacled to a rock, the dragon rising from the waters at her feet. Perseus is depicted flying through the air to her assistance, with unsheathed sword. The design is wholly different from that of the Waite pack.—I.R. [Israel Regardie])

The colors are orange, violet, purplish gray and pearl gray. The flashing color of orange gives deep vivid blue while the flashing color for violet is golden yellow. The flashing colors may always be introduced if they bring out the essential color meaning more clearly. In practice this card usually signifies sympathetic understanding.

The Chariot

Here we have a symbol of the spirit of man controlling the lower principles, soul and body, and thus passing triumphantly through the astral plane, rising above the clouds of illusion and penetrating to the higher spheres.

The colors amber, silver-gray, blue-gray, and the deep blue violet of the night sky elucidate this symbol. It is the sublimation of the Psyche.

Strength

This also represents the mastery of the lower by the higher. But in this case it is the soul which holds in check the passions, although her feet are still planted on earth, and the dark veil still floats about her head and clings around her. The colors, pale greenish yellow, black, yellowish gray, and reddish amber, suggest the steadfast endurance and fortitude required, but the deep red rose which is the flashing color to the greenish yellow, gives the motive power.

The Hermit

Prudence. These three trumps should be collated in studying them for they represent the three stages of initiation. The man wrapped in hood and mantle, and carrying a lantern to illuminate the Path and a staff to support his footsteps, He is the eternal seeker, the Pilgrim soul. His hood and mantle are the brown of earth, and above him is the night-sky. But the delicate yellow-greens and bluish greens of spring are about him, and spring is in his heart.

Wheel of Fortune

In the Etz Chayim, or the Tree of Life, the Wheel is placed on the Pillar of Mercy, where it forms the principal column linking Netzach to Chesed, Victory to Mercy. It is the revolution of experience and progress, the steps of the Zodiac, the revolving staircase, held in place by the counterchanging influence of Light and Darkness, Time and Eternity - presided over by the Plutonian cynocephalus below, and the Sphinx of Egypt above, the eternal Riddle which can only be solved when we attain liberation. The basic colors of this Trump are blue, violet, deep purple, and blue irradiated by yellow. But the zodiacal spokes of the wheel should be in the colors of the spectrum, while the Ape is in those of Malkuth, and the Sphinx in the primary colors and black.

Justice

Nephthys, the third aspect of Luna, the twin sister of Isis. Justice as distinguished from love. Her emblems are the Sword and the Scales. Like her sister, she is clothed in green, but in a sharper, colder green than the pure emerald of Isis. Her subsidiary colors are blue, blue-green, pale green. It is only by utilizing the flashing colors that we can find the hidden warmth and steadfastness.

The Hanged Man

An elusive, because a profoundly significant, symbol. It is sacrifice—the submergence of the higher in the lower in order to sublimate the lower. It is the descent of the Spirit into Matter, the incarnation of God in man, the submission to the nods of matter that the material may be transcended and transmuted. The colors are deep blue, white, and black intermingled but not merged, olive, green, and greenish fawn.

Death

The sign of transmutation and disintegration. The skeleton which alone survives the destructive power of time, may be regarded as the foundation upon which the structure is built, the type which persists through the permutations of Time and Space, adaptable to the requirements of evolution and yet radically unchanged; the transmuting power of Nature working from below upwards, as the Hanged Man is the transmuting power of the spirit working from above downwards. The colors are blue-green, both dark and pale, the two dominant colors of the visible world, and the flashing colors of orange and orange-red.

Temperance

This is the equilibrium not of the balance of Libra, but of the impetus of the Arrow, Sagittarius, which cleaves its way through the air by the force imparted to it by the taut string of the Bow. It requires the counterchanged forces of Fire and Water, Shin and Qoph, held by the restraining power of Saturn, and concentrated by the energies of Mars to initiate this impetus. All these are summed up in the symbolism of the figure standing between Earth and Water, holding two amphorae with their streams of living water, and with the volcano in the background. The colors are bright blue, blue-gray, slate-blue, and lilac-gray.

The Devil

This card should be studied in conjunction with No. 13. They are the two great controlling forces of the Universe, the centrifugal and the centripetal, destructive and reproductive, dynamic and static. The lower nature of man fears and hates the transmuting process; hence the chains binding the lesser figures and the bestial forms of their lower limbs. Yet this very fear of change and disintegration is necessary to stabilize the life-force and preserve continuity. The colors are indigo, livid brown, golden brown and gray.

The Tower

As always red remains persistent throughout the four planes, although modified in tone. Thus we find vivid scarlet shading into deep somber red and vermillion shot with amber. The contrasting shades of green serve to throw the red into relief. The tremendous destructive influence of the lightning, rending asunder established forms to make way for new forms to emerge, revolution as distinguished from transmutation or sublimation, the destructive as opposed to the conservative, energy attacking inertia, the impetuous ejection of those who would enclose themselves in the walls of ease and tradition.

The Star

This shows the seven-pointed Star of Venus shining above the Waters of Aquarius, the guiding force of love in all its forms and aspects, illuminates the soul during her immersion in Humanity, so that the bonds of Saturn are dissolved in the purified Waters of Baptism. The dove of the Spirit hovers above the Tree of Knowledge giving the promise of ultimate attainment - and on the other side gleams of the Tree of Life.

Pale colors suggest dawn and the morning Star—amethyst, pale gray, fawn, dove color and white, with the pale yellow of the Star.

The Moon

Here also is a river but it is the troubled waters of Night, wherein is to be described a crayfish, counterpart of the Scarabeus. It is guarded by the threatening watchgods, seeking to intimidate the wayfarers, while in the distance the barren hills are surmounted by the frowning fortresses still further guarding the way to attainment. It is the path of blood and tears in which fear, weakness, and fluctuation must be overcome. The colors are dark crimson, reddish brown, brownish crimson and plum colors—but their somber hues are lightened by the translucent faint greens and yellows to be found in their counterparts.

The Sun

The Watery Paths of trial and probation are counterbalanced by the fiery paths of Temptation, Judgment, and Decision. In violent contrast to the somber coloring of Aquarius and Pisces, we are confronted by the flaring hues of the Sun and Fire. The too-aspiring Icarus may find his waxen wings of Ambition and Curiosity shriveled and melted by the fiery rays of the Sun and the heat of Fire, but approached with approached with humility and reverence, the Sun becomes the beneficent source of life.

Protected by an enclosing wall, standing by the Waters of repentance, the Pilgrim may submit himself humbly but without fear to the searching Light and absorb warmth and vitality from it for the struggle before him. The colors are clear-orange, golden-yellow, amber shot with red, and the contrasting blue and purple.

The Last Judgment

The three trumps attributed to the Elemental Paths are perhaps the most difficult to understand. They represent the action of forces exterior to the experience of humanity, not the influence of environment but the impact of the Supernals upon the sublunary.

In the Air we have pure spirit holding in leash the lust of the flesh. In water, the sublimating power of sacrifice. Here in Fire, we are shown the cosmic forces concentrating on the pilgrim from all sides. Judgment is pronounced upon him. He is not the judge nor does decision rest in his hands. Lazarus cannot emerge from the Sepulcher until the voice cries out, "Come forth!" Nor can he cast aside the conflicting grave-clothes until the command, "Loose him!" is given. Man of himself is helpless. The impulse to ascend must come from above, but by its power he may transcend the sepulcher of environment and cast aside the trammels of desire. Here once more, the fiery energy of red burns through the planes. Fiery scarlet, glowing crimson, burning red are emphasized by the passive greens.

The Universe

Observe that this represents not the World but the Universe. It should be remembered that to the ancients, Saturn represented the confines of the Solar system. They had no means of measuring either Uranus or Neptune. To them, therefore, Saturn passing through the spiral path of the Zodiac, marked at its cardinal points by the symbols of the Kerubim forming the Cross, was a comprehensive glyph of the whole.

Thus, in this card, we find a synthesis of the whole Taro or Rota. The central figure should be taken as Hathor, Athor, or Ator, rather than Isis, thus indicating the hidden anagram which may perhaps be translated thus: ORAT—man prays, ATOR—to the Great Mother, TARO—who turns, ROTA—the wheel of Life and Death.

The colors like those of the Wheel of Fortune include the colors of the Spectrum and those of the elements, but they are placed against the indigo and black of a Saturn, with the white gleam of the Stars shining in the darkness and the misty figure of the Aimah Elohim in the midst. In the practical Tarot, this card is taken to signify the matter in hand, that is the subject of any question that has been asked.

☽ ☾

Having now revised the 22 Atous or Trumps in succession, it will be wise for the student to reverse the process and seek to follow the Path of the Pilgrim from below upwards, thus seeking to comprehend the interior process of Initiation and Illumination. It is a process in which the whole Universe does not disdain to take part, for Man is himself the Microcosm of the Macrocosm, and the Child of the Gods. And again, the Macrocosm must itself undergoing a corresponding process in which the experience not only of humanity but of each individual must be an integral part. The fragments are gathered up into the baskets, that nothing may be lost; and from the feeding of the multitude there remains not less but more than the unbroken bread and fish - fit emblems of Earth and Water.

Cease not to seek day and night the Purifying Mysteries.

The Bornless Ritual

The Bornless Ritual *is Samuel Liddell Mathers' translation of a ritual from the Greek Magical Papyri, otherwise known as* The Headless One. *The original appeared sometime around the 2nd century C.E. It is an incredibly powerful syncretric ritual that many have found useful in attaining Knowledge and Conversation with their Holy Guardian Angel.*

ಙ ಡ

Thee I invoke, the Bornless one.
Thee, that didst create the Earth and the Heavens:
Thee, that didst create the Night and the Day.
Thee, that didst create the Darkness and the Light.
Thou art Osorronophris: Whom no man has seen at any time.
Thou art Jäbas
Thou art Jäpos:
Thou hast distinguished between the Just and the Unjust.
Thou didst make the Female and the Male.
Thou didst produce the Seed and the Fruit.
Thou didst form Men to love one another, and to hate one another.

I am Mosheh Thy Prophet, unto Whom Thou didst commit Thy Mysteries, the Ceremonies of Ishrael:

Thou didst produce the moist and the dry, and that which nourisheth all created Life.

Hear Thou Me, for I am the Angel of Paphro Osorronophris: this is Thy True Name, handed down to the Prophets of Ishrael.

ಙ ಡ

Hear Me: —
Ar: Thiao: Rheibet: Atheleberseth:
A: Blatha: Abeu: Ebeu: Phi:
Thitasoe: Ib: Thiao.

Hear Me, and make all Spirits subject unto Me: so that every Spirit of the Firmament and of the Ether; upon the Earth and under the Earth: on dry Land and in the Water: of Whirling Air, and of rushing Fire: and every Spell and Scourge of God may be obedient unto Me.

ೞ ଓ

I invoke Thee, the Terrible and Invisible God: Who dwellest in the Void Place of the Spirit.

Arogogorobrao: Sothou:
Modorio: Phalarthao: Doo: Ape, The Bornless One:
Hear Me: etc.

ೞ ଓ

Hear me: —
Roubriao: Mariodam: Balbnabaoth: Assalonai: Aphniao: I: Thoteth: Abrasar: Aeoou: Ischure,
Mighty and Bornless One!
Hear me: etc.

ೞ ଓ

I invoke thee: —
Ma: Barraio: Joel: Kotha:
Athoribalo: Abraoth:
Hear Me: etc.

ೞ ଓ

Hear me!
Aoth: Abaoth: Basum: Isak:
Sabaoth: Iao:

ೞ ଓ

This is the Lord of the Gods:

This is the Lord of the Universe:
This is He Whom the Winds fear.

This is He, Who having made Voice by His Commandment, is Lord of All Things; King, Ruler and Helper. Hear Me, etc.

Hear Me.

Ieou: Pur: Iou: Pur: Iaot: Iaeo: Ioou: Abrasar: Sabriam: Do: Uu: Adonaie: Ede: Edu: Angelos ton Theon: Aniaia Lai: Gaia: Ape: Diathanna Thorun.

I am He! the Bornless Spirit! having sight in the feet: Strong, and the Immortal Fire! I am He! the Truth!
I am He! Who hate that evil should be wrought in the World!
I am He, that lighteneth and thundereth.
I am He, from Whom is the Shower of the Life of Earth: I am He, Whose mouth ever flameth:
I am He, the Begetter and Manifester unto the Light:
I am He; the Grace of the World:

"The Heart Girt with a Serpent" is My Name

Come Thou forth, and follow Me: and make all Spirits subject unto Me so that every Spirit of the, Firmament, and of the Ether: upon the Earth and under the Earth: on dry Land, or in the Water: of whirling Air or of rushing Fire: and every Spell and Scourge of God, may be obedient unto Me!

Iao: Sabao:

Such are the Words!

The Thirty-Two Paths of Wisdom

The earliest texts on Jewish Mysticism refer to 32 Paths of Wisdom. These 32 Paths refer to the 10 Sephirot and the 22 letters of the Hebrew Aleph-bet. (See figure 3 on page 24 and the chapters on the Middle Pillar, Tarot, and Pathworking for more information.) The first path corresponds with the first sephirah, or Keter; the second with Chokmah; and so on to the tenth with Malkhut. The 11th Path corresponds with the first letter: Aleph, which corresponds with the Fool in the Tarot. The 12th path corresponds with Bet or the Magician, and so on to the 32nd path corresponding with the last letter, Tav, which is related to the World or Universe card. This document of unknown origin was translated by William Wynn Westcott—one of the founders of the original Order of the Golden Dawn—and served as part of the inspiration for their Tarot and ritual. It can be particularly helpful for Pathworking and other forms of meditation.

୫୦ ୦୪

The First Path is called the Admirable or the Concealed Intelligence (The Highest Crown) – for it is the Light giving the power of comprehension of that First Principle which has no beginning, and it is the Primal Glory, for no created being can attain to its essence.

The Second Path is that of the Illuminating Intelligence. It is the Crown of Creation, the Splendor of the Unity, equaling it, and it is exalted above every bead, and named by the Kabbalists the Second Glory.

The Third Path is the Sanctifying Intelligence, and is the basis of foundation of Primordial Wisdom, which is called the Former of faith, and its roots, Amen; and it is the parent of Faith, from which virtues doth Faith emanate.

The Fourth Path is named Measuring, Cohesive, or Receptacular; and is so called because it contains all the holy powers, and from it emanate all the spiritual virtues with the most exalted essences: they emanate one from the other by the power of the primordial emanation (The Highest Crown), blessed be it.

The Fifth Path is called the Radical Intelligence, because it is itself the essence equal to the Unity, uniting itself to the BINAH or Intelligence which emanates from the primordial depths of Wisdom or CHOCHMAH.

The Sixth Path is called the Intelligence of the Mediating Influence, because in it are multiplied the influxes of the emanations; for it causes that affluence to flow into all the reservoirs of the Blessings, with which these themselves are united.

The Seventh Path is the Occult Intelligence, because it is the Refulgent Splendor of all the Intellectual virtues which are perceived by the eyes of intellect, and by the contemplation of faith.

The Eighth Path is called Absolute or Perfect, because it is the means of the primordial, which has no root by which it can cleave, nor rest, except in the hidden places of GEDULAH. Magnificence, which emanate from its own proper essence.

The Ninth Path is the Pure intelligence so called because it purifies the Numerations, it proves and corrects the designing of their representation, and disposes their unity with which they are combined without diminution or division.

The Tenth Path is the Resplendent Intelligence, because it is exalted above every bead, and sits on the throne of BINAH (the Intelligence spoken of in the Third Path). It illuminates the splendor of all lights, and causes a supply of influence to emanate from the Prince of countenances.

The Eleventh Path is the Scintillating Intelligence because it is the essence of that curtain which is placed close to the order of the disposition, and this is a special dignity given to it that it may be able to stand before the Face of the Cause of Causes.

The Twelfth Path is the Intelligence of Transparency, because it is that species of Magnificence, called CHAZCHAZIT, which is named the place whence issues the vision of those seeing in apparitions. (That is, the prophecies by seers in a vision.)

The Thirteenth Path is named the Uniting Intelligence and is so called because it is itself the essence of Glory. It is the Consummation of the Truth of individual spiritual things.

The Fourteenth Path is the Illuminating Intelligence, and is so called because it is itself that CHASHMAL which is the founder of the concealed and fundamental ideas of holiness and of their stages of preparation.

The Fifteenth Path is the Constituting Intelligence, so called because it constitutes the substance of creation in pure darkness, and men have spoken of these contemplations; it is that darkness spoken of in scripture, Job xxxviii. 9, "and thick darkness a swaddling band for it."

The Sixteenth Path is the Triumphal or Eternal Intelligence, so called because it is the pleasure of the Glory, beyond which is no other Glory like to it, and it is called also the Paradise prepared for the Righteous.

The Seventeenth Path is the Disposing Intelligence, which provides Faith to the Righteous, and they are clothed with the Holy Spirit by it, and it is called the Foundation of Excellence in the state of higher thing.

The Eighteenth Path is called the House of Influence (by the greatness of whose abundance the influx of good things upon created beings is increased) and from the midst of the investigation the arcana and hidden senses are drawn forth, which dwell in its shade and which cling to it, from the cause of all causes.

The Nineteenth Path is the Intelligence of all the activities of the spiritual beings, and is so called because of the affluence diffused by it from the most high blessing and most exalted sublime glory.

The Twentieth Path is the Intelligence of Will, and is so called because it is the means of preparation of all and each created being, and by this intelligence the existence of the Primordial Wisdom becomes known.

The Twenty-first Path is the Intelligence of Conciliation, and is so called because it receives the divine influence which flows into it from its benediction upon all and each existence.

The Twenty-second Path is the Faithful Intelligence, and is so called because by it spiritual virtues are increased, and all dwellers on earth are nearly under its shadow.

The Twenty-third Path is the Stable Intelligence, and it is so called because it has the virtue of consistency among all numerations.

The Twenty-fourth Path is the Imaginative Intelligence, and it is so called because it gives a likeness to all the similitudes, which are created in like manner similar to its harmonious elegancies.

The Twenty-fifth Path is the Intelligence of Probation, or is Tentative, and is so called because it is the primary temptation, by which the Creator (blessed be He) trieth all righteous persons.

The Twenty-sixth Path is called the Renovating Intelligence, because the Holy God (blessed be He) renews by it, all the changing things which are renewed by the creation of the world.

The Twenty-seventh Path is the Exciting Intelligence, and it is so called bemuse by it is created the Intellect of all created beings under the highest heaven, and the excitement or motion of them.

The Twenty-eighth Path is the Natural Intelligence, and is so called because through it is consummated and perfected the nature of every existent being under the orb of the Sun, in perfection.

The Twenty-ninth Path is the Corporeal Intelligence, so called because it forms every body which is, formed beneath the whole set of worlds and the increment of them.

The Thirtieth Path is the Collecting Intelligence, and is so called because Astrologers deduce from it the judgment of the Stars, and of the celestial signs, and the perfections of their science, according to the rules of their revolutions.

The Thirty-first Path is the Perpetual Intelligence; and why is it so called? Because it regulates the motions of the Sun and Moon in their proper order, each in an orbit convenient for it.

The Thirty-second Path is the Administrative Intelligence, and it is so called because it directs and associates, in all their operations, the seven planets, even all of them in their own due courses.

www.ingramcontent.com/pod-product-compliance
Lightning Source LLC
Chambersburg PA
CBHW031145160426
43193CB00008B/259